PRESENTED
BY THE
QUEEN

The Crimea Medal Award Ceremony,
18th May, 1855.

Compiled by

Neil Mitchell and Peter Duckers

◆JADE◆

Jade Publishing Limited,
5, Leefields Close, Uppermill, Oldham, Lancashire, OL3 6LA.

This first edition published by Jade Publishing Limited 1996.

© Kingswood Books 1996
   All rights reserved.

ISBN 1 900734 06 0 Presented by the Queen. (Pbk).

Printed in Great Britain by
Taylor & Clifton Limited, Uppermill, Oldham, Lancashire.

Typeset by
Jade Publishing Limited, Uppermill, Oldham, Lancashire.

A CIP catalogue record for this book is available
from the British Library

Her Majesty Queen Victoria presenting the Crimea Medal to Lieut. Colonel Sir Thomas Troubridge at the award ceremony at the Horse Guards, 18th May, 1855. She also graciously bestowed the honour of being Her Aide de Camp on the maimed veteran, who had lost both his feet at the battle of Inkermann.

Contents

Acknowledgments

We should like to thank Mr. Murray Shaw and Mr. Peter Fisher for information on medals in their collections. For valued help and additional material our thanks are due to Mr. Ian Laidler and Mr. Ian McInnes.

Neil Mitchell and Peter Duckers, 1996.

The Crimea Medal Ceremony

On 18th May, 1855, Queen Victoria presided over the first ceremony in which a reigning monarch presented campaign medals to her soldiers and sailors. As the war was still in progress, it stands to reason that the bulk of Her Majesty's Army and Navy engaged against the Russians was still at the seat of war in the Crimea, the Black Sea and the Baltic, so that the majority of the officers and other ranks of the Army, Marines and Navy who were presented with medals were home on leave or because of wounds or illness. Many of them were to return to the Crimea after the ceremony; there are one or two cases of men being present who had not yet served in the Crimea and others who never did.

Although originally intended to be a simple ceremony to honour as many men as could be assembled from every regiment in the army which had fought at the Alma, Balaklava and Inkermann, it was soon transformed into a major national and social event. Extensive galleries, covered with crimson cloth, were built at strategic points around the Horse Guards to house spectators drawn from members of the Government (including Lord Palmerston, the Duke of Newcastle and W.E. Gladstone), the Houses of Commons and Lords, high-ranking families, families of the officers and men to be honoured and members of the public who flocked to witness the ceremony in their thousands, though the general public fared badly in the allocation of viewing space. The roofs of the nearby buildings of the Horse Guards, the Admiralty and the Treasury were equally crowded with interested onlookers. The magnificence of the occasion was enhanced by the hundreds of soldiers on parade, in addition to the recipients, in the colourful full-dress of just about every regiment, regular and volunteer, in the army along with the Royal Marines and Royal

1

Navy. Many of the officers and men were wearing their orders, decorations and medals. The Queen and Prince Consort were to be seated on gilded chairs on a crimson-draped dias about 50 yards from the Horse Guards, facing St. James's Park.

The troops who were to line the parade ground for the ceremony assembled at 9.00a.m. and consisted of:

Grenadier Guards	- four flank companies.
Coldstream Guards	- two flank companies.
Scots Fusilier Guards	- two flank companies.
1st Life Guards	- 1st Squadron.
2nd Life Guards	- 1st Squadron.
Royal Horse Guards	- 1st Squadron, Blues.
6th Dragoon Guards	- 1st Squadron.

The officers and men waiting to receive their medals were drawn up behind the Foot Guards (between them and St. James's Park) along with other representatives of the regiments in the Crimea. Those who were to receive the medals from the Queen were placed to the right of the group, arranged in numerical order of regiment from left to right.

Once these units and recipients had been placed, at 9.30a.m., the band of the Royal Marines marched on to the Horse Guards followed by the officers and men of the Royal Navy and Royal Marines who were to receive awards. They were positioned to the right of the Royal dias, near the Admiralty.

The whole parade came under the command of the Duke of Cambridge on his arrival at 10.00a.m. and shortly after, the Royal entourage arrived, accompanied by a panoply of high-ranking military and naval officers, which included the Commander-in-Chief, Lord Hardinge, General Lord Gough, Major General Lord Lucan, the Earl of Cardigan, Major General

Sir John Scarlett and the Minister for War, Lord Panmure. The Queen herself, accompanied amongst others by Prince Albert and the Prince of Wales, entered the Parade from Whitehall at 11.00a.m., to cheers from the crowds of spectators and an artillery salute. The presentation of the medals began almost immediately.

Recipients were marched to the front and halted in line about 100 feet from the Royal dias, in regimental order of precedence. As the regimental bands played appropriate music, the officers and men then passed before the Queen in single file. As each one approached the left of the royal dias, he handed to the Adjutant General, Major General Weatherall, a card with his name, rank and details of wounds, if any. These details were read out by General Weatherall for the Queen and attendants to hear. The medals were passed to the Queen by the Minister of War standing to her right, and she, in turn, handed them to the officer or man whose name had just been read out, occasionally asking them a question about their services or expressing sympathy for their wounds. The first recipient of the medal was the Duke of Cambridge, followed by Colonel MacDonald, A.D.C. to the Duke, then Lord Lucan, the Earl of Cardigan, Sir James Scarlett, the members of their Staffs, and then the officers and men of the Cavalry, Corps and Infantry.

Many of the men presented were visibly suffering from the effects of wounds or illness and were on crutches, sticks or in wheel-chairs or were helped along by friends; these received special cheers from the crowd and none more so than Lieut. Colonel Sir Thomas Troubridge of the 7th Regiment who had lost both feet in action. The Queen, in addition to handing Sir Thomas his medal, conferred upon him the position of A.D.C. to Her Majesty. Other severely wounded officers who attracted universal sympathy were Captain Frederic Sayer, 23rd Regiment, and Captain Currie of the 19th, one in a wheel chair and one on crutches.

The presentation to the officers and men of the Royal Navy and Royal Marines followed that to the members of the army, with Vice Admiral Dundas the first to receive the medal, followed by the officers and men in descending order of rank. The Royal Marines were the last to receive the awards. It then remained only to close the proceedings and march the regiments and detachments off to their various quarters. The royal entourage left by carriage for Buckingham Palace via the Mall; the non-commissioned recipients of medals marched to the Queen's Riding School at Pimlico to a celebration lunch, where they were later visited by the Queen, Prince Albert and the Prince of Wales and other Royal personages and escorts.

"The Times" published an account of the proceedings on Saturday 19th May, 1855, as did *"The Illustrated London News"* on Saturday 26th May, 1855.

The Medal Roll

The compilers have put together a complete roll of the officers and men who were presented with the Crimea Medal by Queen Victoria on 18th May, 1855. The recipients are identified on the Crimea Medal Roll at the Public Record Office, Kew, and in various local and national newspapers, such as *"The Times"*. The lists which follow are intended purely and simply to offer a ready means of identifying those individuals who received their medal from the Queen at the Horse Guards. Where possible, we have added details of medal entitlement, wounds, promotions and other awards specifically for service in the Crimean War. We have by no means attempted to fill out the full details of the careers and war services of officers and other ranks, which are available in several sources for those interested in researching the careers of individuals. For example, see Army and Navy Lists, published rolls and lists (such as those of Kane, Lummis & Wynn and Abbott), service papers in the W.O.97 series in the P.R.O., and others.

The compilers have examined about a dozen medals to men named in the roll and although this represents only a very small proportion of the whole, it is notable that all are named in the same style *viz.* small engraved upright capitals, which give the recipient's rank, full name and regiment. It may be that the medals were all named prior to the ceremony, ready for presentation, and that all will be found named in the same style. The compilers would be interested to hear from any collector who may own or see one of the medals "presented by the Queen" to compare the naming styles.

There are one or two recipients to whom "duplicate" awards are known, the "second" medal being named in impressed capitals; could it be that these were recipients who returned to the Crimea after the ceremony and were included on a subsequent medal roll? There also seem to be instances of men present at the Horse Guards' ceremony on 18th May, who had not, in fact, been to the Crimea by that date. Were they given medals with no clasp? More interestingly, there are cases of recipients of medals "presented by the Queen" for whom no Crimean War service can be traced at all. Examples are Major H.A. Turner and Captain G.H.J.A. Fraser, both of the Royal Artillery. Neither Kane's *"List"* nor later Army Lists indicate any service in the Crimea by these two men. Similar examples are Midshipmen M.B. Medlycott and N.S.F. Digby, R.N. What were these men given at the ceremony?

Sources Consulted:

"The London Gazette".
"The Times".
Army and Navy Lists.
Kane's List of Officers of the Royal Artillery, 1716-1899: Clowes & Son, London 1900.
Honour the Light Brigade: W.M.Lummis & K.G.Wynn, Hayward, London 1963.
Returns Relating to Officers in the Army (Crimea): Wm. Ewart, London 1857.
Crimean War Casualty Roll: F. & A. Cook, Hayward, London 1976.
Recipients of the Distinguished Conduct Medal, 1855-1909: P.E. Abbott, London 1975.
Medals of the British Army: Thos. Carter & W.H. Long, 1893; Reprint, 1973.

Alphabetical List
of Recipients.

Crimea Medals presented by the Queen.

The alphabetical list of the Officers and Other Ranks of the Army, the Royal Navy and the Royal Marines who were personally presented with the Crimea medal by Her Majesty Queen Victoria in the ceremony at the Royal Horse Guards on 18th May, 1855.

An asterisk (*) by a name indicates that the recipient's medal is known to exist.

Abbott, Frederick Tydd.	Assistant Surgeon.	41st Regiment.
Adam, Charles.	Private.	2nd Dragoons.
Adams, Allen Crosby.	Midshipman.	Royal Navy.
Adams, John M.	Private.	20th Regiment.
Agnew, James.	Captain.	39th Regiment.
Amherst, W.A., the Hon.	Captain.	1st Cold. Guards.
Anderson, James.	Private.	79th Regiment.
Anderson, T.E.	Lieut. (Riding Master)	6th Dragoons.
Anderson, Warren H.	Lieutenant.	Royal Navy.
Angel, John.	Private.	Royal Marines.
Annesley, H., the Hon.	Lieutenant.	1st Scots Fus. Gds.
Annesley, Wm. Richard.	Captain.	97th Regiment.
Armstrong, Ed. Marcus.	Captain.	55th Regiment.
Ashkettle, James.	Private.	1st Cold. Guards.
Astley, Richard D.	Captain.	49th Regiment.
Austin, Thomas.	Colour Sergeant.	1st Cold. Guards.
Baddeley, J.F.Lodington.	Major.	Royal Artillery.
Bagshaw, James.	Gunner/Driver.	Royal Artillery.
Bamford, Robert Carter.	Captain.	63rd Regiment.
Barfelt, Thomas.	Sergeant.	Royal Artillery.
Baring, Charles.*	Captain.	1st Cold. Guards.
Barnard, Emanuel.	Private.	1st Cold. Guards.
Barnes, Samuel.*	Private.	Royal Marines.
Barnston, William.	Captain.	55th Regiment.
Barrack, William	Private.	7th Regiment.
Barrett, Richard Doyle.*	Captain.	19th Regiment.
Barstow, George.	Major.	Royal Artillery.
Batchelor, Henry.	Colour Sergeant.	Royal Marines.
Bates, William.	Private.	Royal Marines.
Bathurst, H.	Captain.	23rd Regiment.

11

Bayly, P.	Brevet Major.	30th Regiment.
Baynes, H.J. Le M.	Captain.	88th Regiment.
Bazalgette, E.	Lieutenant.	95th Regiment.
Beard, John.	Able Seaman.	Royal Navy.
Beaumont, Godfrey W.	Lieutenant.	1st Scots Fus. Gds.
Beechey, J.	Private.	23rd Regiment.
Beer, J.	Armourer.	Royal Navy.
Berkeley, C.A.	Lieutenant Colonel.	1st Scots Fus. Gds.
Berkeley, Joshua.	Lieutenant.	Royal Navy.
Beswick, J.	Captain.	38th Regiment.
Bevan, Samuel.	Private.	1st Regiment.
Beveridge, Hugh T.S.	Doctor; Surgeon.	Royal Navy.
Biddlecombe, George.	Private.	1st Scots Fus. Gds.
Billington, Thomas.	Gunner/Driver.	Royal Artillery.
Bingham, Chas., Lord.	Captain.	1st Cold. Guards.
Bird, Ed. Timothy B.	Engineer.	Royal Navy.
Bissett, G. Ed. L.C.	Captain.	55th Regiment.
Blenerhasset, Barry.	Captain.	71st Regiment.
Bligh, Fredk. C.	Captain.	41st Regiment.
Board, George.	Private.	Royal Marines.
Boden, John.	Private.	68th Regiment.
Boldero, George Neeld.	Brevet Major.	21st Regiment.
Boot, John E.	Gunner/Driver.	Royal Artillery.
Boothby, Basil Charles.	Lieutenant.	95th Regiment.
Borrett, Thomas.	Lieutenant.	Royal Navy.
Borthwick, Charles.	Private.	79th Regiment.
Boulton, Wm. R.	Lieutenant.	Royal Navy.
Bourchier, Claud T.	Captain.	Rifle Brigade.
Boyd, William.	Private.	1st Scots Fus. Gds.
Boyle, William George.	the Hon. Captain.	1st Cold. Guards.
Bradford, M.	Lieutenant.	44th Regiment.
Bradford, Ralph.	Lieutenant Colonel.	Grenadier Guards.
Bradford, Wilmot H.	Lieutenant Colonel.	Rifle Brigade.
Bradshaw [-].	Private.	21st Regiment.
Bredin, Edgar G.	Captain.	Royal Artillery.
Breeze, John.	Sergeant.	11th Hussars.
Bremner, John T.U.	Medical Officer.	Royal Navy.
Brendon, Algernon.	Captain.	Royal Artillery.
Bridge, Wm. Henry.	Commander.	Royal Navy.
Bridges, Frederick.	Corporal.	1st Cold. Guards.
Bridget, H.	Chief Quartermaster.	Royal Navy.
Brinckman, T.	Captain.	17th Regiment.
Brooks, Charles.	Admiral's Coxswain.	Royal Navy.
Brown, [-].	Acting Comm. Clk.	Commissariat Dept.

Brown(e), Andrew.	Brevet Lieut. Colonel.	44th Regiment.
Brown, Ed. J. Vesey.	Major.	88th Regiment.
Brown, John.	Private.	6th Dragoons.
Brown, Samuel.	Private.	77th Regiment.
Brown, Thos. S.	Captain.	55th Regiment.
Brown, Thomas.	Chief Quartermaster.	Royal Navy.
Brown, William.	Quartermaster Sergeant.	Royal Artillery.
Bull, James.	Lieutenant.	Royal Navy.
Bull, John.	Private.	90th Regiment.
Buller, Coote.	Captain.	Rifle Brigade.
Buller, James Hornby.	Lieutenant.	57th Regiment.
Bulwer, Ed. G.	Captain.	23rd Regiment.
Bunton, John.	Private.	Royal Marines.
Burgoyne, J. M., Sir	Captain.	Grenadier Guards.
Burrell, William.	Private.	1st Cold. Guards.
Burt, John.	Private.	1st Cold. Guards.
Burton, William.	Private.	33rd Regiment.
Burtonwood, P. [?Chas.]	Private.	1st Cold. Guards.
Bush, Benjamin.	Private.	Royal Marines.
Bush, Henry Stratton.	Captain.	41st Regiment.
Bush, Henry.	Gunner/Driver.	Royal Artillery.
Butler, H.W.P.	Captain.	7th Regiment.
Bye, Richard.	Sergeant.	1st Scots Fus. Gds.
Cahill, Patrick.	Lieutenant.	49th Regiment.
Cambridge, the Duke of.	Colonel.	Staff.
Cameron, A.	Lieutenant Colonel.	42nd Regiment.
Cameron, W.G.	Major.	Grenadier Guards.
Campbell, A.C.	Brevet Major.	42nd Regiment.
Capel, R.A., Hon.	Lieutenant.	Royal Navy.
Carden, Henry R.	Captain.	77th Regiment.
Cardigan, the Earl of.	Major General.	Staff.
Careless, William.	Private 2557.	Rifle Brigade.
Carey, William.	Private.	28th Regiment.
Carnay, [-].	Private.	5th Dragoon Gds.
Carney, William.	Private.	44th Regiment.
Carpenter, G.W.W.	Captain.	7th Regiment.
Carpenter, [-].	Captain.	Staff.
Carthew, George.	Staff Wheeler.	Royal Artillery.
Cator, John.	Lieutenant.	68th Regiment.
Cecil, Edward, Lord.	Lieutenant.	Royal Navy.
Charlton, Ed. Spicer.	Captain.	95th Regiment.
Chase, William.	Corporal.	Royal Marines.
Chetwynd, H.W., Hon.	Lieutenant.	Royal Navy.
Chun, Joseph.	Private.	95th Regiment.

Clark, William.	Corporal.	11th Hussars.
Clatworthy, William.	Private.	1st Cold. Guards.
Clay, George, Sir.	Captain.	19th Regiment.
Clayhills, J.M.	Lieutenant.	93rd Regiment.
Clifton, Thos. Henry.	Captain.	Staff.
Climpston, William.	Private.	Royal Marines.
Coachman, William.	Driver.	Royal Artillery.
Coakley, Daniel.	Gunner's Mate.	Royal Navy.
Coats, John.	Major.	55th Regiment.
Cockburn, J.	Captain.	63rd Regiment.
Coleman, Ryan.	Private 2804.	49th Regiment.
Coles, Richard G.	Captain.	1st Regiment.
Coney, P.G.	Captain.	7th Regiment.
Connally, John.	Private.	4th Regiment.
Conolly, James.	Captain.	Staff.
Copeland, Alex L.	Captain.	57th Regiment.
Corban, Wm. Watts.	Captain.	49th Regiment.
Cornes, John.	Paymaster.	79th Regiment.
Court, Thomas.	Private.	7th Regiment.
Cox, Edmund H.	Lieutenant.	Royal Marines.
Coy, Robert.	Bombardier.	Royal Artillery.
Coyle, J.	Private.	9th Regiment.
Craster, J. Thomas.	Captain.	38th Regiment.
Craw, John.	Sergeant.	1st Scots Fus. Gds.
Crawford, William.	Sergeant.	Royal Artillery.
Creighton, Robert.	Assistant Surgeon.	Royal Navy.
Cresswell, George.	Lieutenant.	89th Regiment.
Crichton, R. Orr.	Assistant Surgeon.	4th Light Dragns.
Crofton, A., Hon.	Lieutenant.	7th Regiment.
Cromwell, Matthew.	Private.	77th Regiment.
Cross, Charles.	Sergeant 1866.	47th Regiment.
Cross, Robert.	Sergeant.	49th Regiment.
Crosse, Joshua G.	Captain.	88th Regiment.
Crowe, William.	Sergeant.	Royal Artillery.
Crowley, Jeremiah.	Private.	33rd Regiment.
Cruse, G.	Lieutenant.	1st Royal Dragns.
Cunningham, John.	Corporal 3041.	49th Regiment.
Cunningham, W.	Captain.	79th Regiment.
Currie, L.D. Hay.	Captain.	19th Regiment.
D'Aguilar, Chas. L.	Major.	Royal Artillery.
D'Arcy, O.C.	Staff Surgeon.	
Dacres, S. Colpoys.	Captain.	Royal Navy.
Dallas, H.	Captain.	11th Hussars.
Dalrymple, John H.E.	Lieutenant Colonel.	1st Scots Fus. Gds.

14

Daly, Patrick.	Sergeant.	19th Regiment.
Dalzell, R.A.G.	Lieut. Colonel.	63rd Regiment.
Damer, S.	Captain.	1st Scots Fus. Gds.
Dashwood, H.W.	Captain.	Royal Artillery.
Davis, John.	Gunner/Driver.	Royal Artillery.
Dawe, W.	Armourer.	Royal Navy.
Dawson, E.S.F.G.	Captain.	93rd Regiment.
Day, Joseph.	Able Seaman.	Royal Navy.
Day, Martin.	Private.	88th Regiment.
De Havilland, James.	Captain.	Royal Artillery.
De Horsey, Wm. H.B.	Major.	Grenadier Guards.
Deedes, William.	Captain.	Rifle Brigade.
Dickson, G.	Brevet Major.	30th Regiment.
Digby, N.S. Fox.	Midshipman.	Royal Navy.
Dillon, Charles.	Corporal.	77th Regiment.
Dimmock, William.*	Corporal.	17th Lancers.
Disney, E.	Lieutenant.	7th Regiment.
Dixon, T.F.	Captain.	39th Regiment.
Dixon, William.	Gunner/Driver.	Royal Artillery.
Doherty, Daniel.	Quartermaster.	38th Regiment.
Drake, G.A. Tyrwhitt.	Lieutenant.	Royal Navy.
Drummond, A.	Captain.	Rifle Brigade.
Drummond, Benjamin.	Private 3718.	1st Scots Fus. Gds.
Dulahan, T.	Private.	Rifle Brigade.
Dumbreck, David.	Doctor.	Medical Staff.
Dundas, J.W.D., Sir.	Vice Admiral.	Royal Navy.
Dunkellin, U.C., Lord.	Lieutenant Colonel.	1st Cold. Guards.
Dunn, Peter.	Corporal.	4th Regiment.
Durrant, Francis.	Midshipman.	Royal Navy.
Earle, William Henry.	Captain.	17th Regiment.
Eden, Charles.	Captain.	Royal Navy.
Edis, John.	Private.	19th Regiment.
Edsell, Henry.	Sergeant.	Royal Marines.
Edwards, John.	Private.	28th Regiment.
Elgney, William.	Sergeant.	Ryl. Marine Artilly.
Elliot, G., the Hon.	Brevet Major.	Rifle Brigade.
Elliott, A.J.H.	Captain.	5th Dragoon Gds.
Elliott, Henry.	Bombardier.	Royal Artillery.
Ellis, George.	Captain.	4th Light Dragns.
Elme, John.	Able Seaman.	Royal Navy.
Elmsall, W. de C.	Captain.	1st Royal Dragns.
Elrington, Fredk. R.	Major.	Rifle Brigade.
Emery, Jonathan.	Private 2594.	1st Scots Fus. Gds.
England, Richard.	Captain.	55th Regiment.

15

Ennismore, Lord.	Captain.	1st Scots Fus. Gds.
Erroll, Wm. H., Earl of.	Brevet Major.	Rifle Brigade.
Ervan, [-].	Private.	93rd Regiment.
Erwin, James.	Private.	63rd Regiment.
Evans, de Lacy, Sir.	Lieuenant General.	Staff.
Evelyn, [-]	Lieutenant Colonel.	Staff. (Turkish).
Ewart, Chas. J. Fredk.	Captain.	Royal Navy.
Ewing, J.	Surgeon on Staff.	Dep. Insp. Genl.
Fairtlough, Chas. Ed.	Captain.	63rd Regiment.
Falkner, Ed. Newstead.	Captain.	30th Regiment.
Fane, J.A.	Captain.	46th Regiment.
Farrel, John.	Private.	55th Regiment.
Farrell, Patrick.	Corporal.	Royal Marines.
Fawckner, Wm. H.	Second Master.	Royal Navy.
Fielding, P.R.B.	Brevet Major.	1st Cold. Guards.
Findley, David.	Driver.	Royal Artillery.
Fitzgerald, Patrick.	Private.	28th Regiment.
FitzGerald, W.H.D.	Captain.	7th Regiment
Fitzroy, A.C.L., Lord.	Lieutenant Colonel.	1st Cold. Guards.
Fitzroy, Cavendish C.	Captain.	68th Regiment.
Fitzroy, George R.	Captain.	1st Cold. Guards.
Fletcher, Charles.	Private.	Royal Marines.
Flood, Ferdinand H.S.	Midshipman.	Royal Navy.
Flower, W.	Assistant Surgeon.	63rd Regiment.
Flynn, Michael.	Bombardier.	Ryl. Marine Artilly.
Forrest, John.	Doctor.	Medical Staff.
Fost, W.	Leading Seaman.	Royal Navy.
Foster, John.	Private.	55th Regiment.
Foulkes, Chas. Kenrick.	Clerk.	Royal Navy.
Fox, Edward.	Private 1324.	55th Regiment.
Fox, George.	Corporal.	42nd Regiment.
France, Robert.	Private.	Royal Marines.
Franklin, Chas. T.	Major.	Royal Artillery.
Fraser, Alexr. E.	Captain.	1st Scots Fus. Gds.
Fraser, G.H.J.A.	Captain.	Royal Artillery.
Freese, J.N.A.	Lieutenant Colonel.	Royal Artillery.
Freme, J.	Captain.	79th Regiment.
Fyffe, W.	Assistant Surgeon.	30th Regiment.
Gaffney, James.	Private.	33rd Regiment.
Gaffney, James.	Private.	63rd Regiment.
Gallagher, Peter.	Private.	47th Regiment.
Gambier, Gloucester.	Lieutenant Colonel.	Royal Artillery.
Garland, James.	Admiral's Coxswain.	Royal Navy.
Garrad, Thomas.	Private.	1st Cold. Guards.

Garrard, R.	Captain.	95th Regiment.
George, Henry.	Private.	44th Regiment.
Gibb, Charles John.	Captain.	Royal Engineers.
Gibbons, Abraham.	Private.	13th Light Dragns.
Gibbs, George.	Gunner/Driver.	Royal Artillery.
Gilborne, Edward.	Assistant Surgeon.	Royal Artillery.
Gillam, David J.	Sergeant 1130.	4th Light Dragns.
Gipps, Reginald.	Captain.	1st Scots Fus. Gds.
Gloster, Edward T.	Captain.	38th Regiment.
Goff, Charles.	Private.	Royal Marines.
Goodall, William.	Corporal.	38th Regiment.
Gooden, Thomas.	Private.	Royal Marines.
Goodman, James.	Gunner/Driver.	Royal Artillery.
Gore-Booth, R.N.	Lieutenant.	4th Light Dragns.
Goss, James.	Private 3201.	46th Regiment.
Gough, T.B.	Brevet Lieut. Colonel.	33rd Regiment.
Gould, Wyndham.	Private.	1st Cold. Guards.
Goulding, John.	Able Seaman.	Royal Navy.
Graham, C.	Captain.	Royal Navy.
Graham, W., Doctor.	Surgeon.	Royal Navy.
Granville, Bevil.	Captain.	23rd Regiment.
Greatrex, Thos. Price.	Cornet.	13th Light Dragns.
Greenwood, John J.	Lieutenant.	33rd Regiment.
Greville, H.F.	Captain.	Royal Navy.
Gribble, James.	Able Seaman.	Royal Navy.
Griffiths, J.F.	Lieutenant.	Royal Navy.
Grimmond, Peter.	Private.	1st Scots Fus. Gds.
Guise, John C.	Captain.	90th Regiment.
Gunter, Robert.	Lieutenant.	4th Dragoon Gds.
Hadley, James.	Private.	1st Cold. Guards.
Hague, Dennis.	Private.	63rd Regiment.
Haines, Fredk. Paul.	Lieutenant Colonel.	21st Regiment.
Hains, John.	Sergeant Major.	Royal Artillery.
Hall, John.	Private.	90th Regiment.
Halpin, Robert.	Reverend.	Chaplain.
Haly, Wm. O'Grady.	Lieutenant Colonel.	47th Regiment.
Hamilton, B.S.	Midshipman.	Royal Navy.
Hamilton, W.	Paymaster.	Royal Navy.
Hannah, Alexander.	Private 3617.	1st Scots Fus. Gds.
Hapgood, George.	Private.	Royal Marines.
Harcourt, J.	Captain.	30th Regiment.
Hardinge, Henry.	Major.	Rifle Brigade.
Harin, Dinnes [Dennis?]	Private.	49th Regiment.
Harries, Thomas.	Major.	63rd Regiment.

17

Hartopp, J.W.C.	Captain.	17th Lancers.
Hartopp, W.W.	Lieutenant.	1st Royal Dragns.
Harvey, Robert.	Sergeant.	1st Cold. Guards.
Haslem, Henry.	Private.	95th Regiment.
Hawkins, Joseph.	Private.	1st Cold. Guards.
Hawkins, Robert.	Bombardier.	Royal Artillery.
Hay, Alex. S. Leith.	Lieut. Colonel.	93rd Regiment.
Hearn, Charles Bush.	Surgeon.	1st Regiment.
Henderson, A.	Lieutenant.	Royal Navy.
Henning, Shurlock.	Captain.	88th Regiment.
Henson, Frederick.	Private.	Royal Marines.
Hewlett, William J.	Gunner.	Ryl. Marine Artilly.
Hibbard, Samuel.	Private.	1st Cold. Guards.
Hicks, Joseph.	Private.	19th Regiment.
Holbrook, John.	Private.	97th Regiment.
Holdaway, Andrew.	Colour Sergeant.	Rifle Brigade.
Holder, H.L.	Lieutenant.	Royal Navy.
Holmes, Joseph.	Gunner/Driver.	Royal Artillery.
Holyer, William.	Lance Corporal.	Royal Marines.
Hooper, John.	Sergeant.	Royal Artillery.
Horsford, Alfred H.	Lieut. Colonel.	Rifle Brigade.
Hoy, John.	Private.	1st Cold. Guards.
Hudson, Daniel.	Private.	55th Regiment.
Hughes, Charles.	Gunner/Driver.	Royal Artillery.
Hume, Henry.	Lieut. Colonel.	95th Regiment.
Hume, Robert.	Captain.	55th Regiment.
Hunter, Robert.	Private.	2nd Dragoons.
Hutchinson, John E.	Private.	Royal Marines.
Hutton, Thomas.	Captain.	4th Light Dragns.
Inglis, T.	Captain.	Rifle Brigade.
Innis, [-].	Farrier.	4th Dragoon Gds.
Irby, L.H. Lloyd.	Lieutenant.	90th Regiment.
Irving, Alexander.	Lieutenant Colonel.	Royal Artillery.
Jackson, James.	Private.	Royal Marines.
James, J.	Captain of Forecastle.	Royal Navy.
Jeffreys, Edmund R.	Lieutenant Colonel.	Staff.
Jennings, G.B.	Captain.	19th Regiment.
Jillard, Jacob.	Leading Seaman.	Royal Navy.
John, G.	Captain.	23rd Regiment.
Johns, T.	Captain.	63rd Regiment.
Johnson, James.	Sergeant.	Rifle Brigade.
Johnston, A.	Assistant Surgeon.	68th Regiment.
Jones, William Gore.	Commander.	Royal Navy.
Joste, J.S.	Carpenter's Crew.	Royal Navy.

Joy, William.	Private.	1st Scots Fus. Gds.
Juggins, William.	Drummer 2912.	1st Scots Fus. Gds.
Kane, [-].	Major.	Staff. (Ind. Army).
Keane, William.	Sergeant.	33rd Regiment.
Keene, John.	Private.	13th Lt. Dragoons.
Keeting, James.	Corporal.	57th Regiment.
Kelly, Patrick.	Private.	88th Regiment.
Kennedy, Robert.	Gunner.	Ryl. Marine Artilly.
Kenrick, Buxton M.	Lieutenant.	33rd Regiment.
Killilea, Thomas.	Private.	88th Regiment.
Kilvert, John.	Sergeant.	11th Hussars.
King, [-].	Assistant Surgeon.	41st Regiment.
King, Ed. Raleigh.	Lieutenant.	13th Light Dragns.
King, John.	Private.	1st Cold. Guards.
Kite, Isaac.	Private.	38th Regiment.
Knollys, W.W.	Captain.	1st Scots Fus. Gds.
Kynaston, A.F.	Captain.	Royal Navy.
Lacey, James.	Private.	1st Cold. Guards.
Lake, Noel Thomas.	Lieutenant Colonel.	Royal Artillery.
Lambe, J.W.	Mate.	Royal Navy.
Lambert, L.	Lieutenant.	Royal Navy.
Land, James.	Private.	50th Regiment.
Lawrenson, John.	Colonel.	17th Lancers.
Lawson, [-].	Corporal.	21st Regiment.
Lawson, David.	Private.	42nd Regiment.
Le Maitre, A.	Acting Commissariat Clk.	Commissariat Dept.
Leet, E.	Captain.	20th Regiment.
Lempriere, G. Reid.	Lieutenant.	Royal Engineers.
Leslie, Thomas.	Lieutenant.	Staff. (R. H. Gds.)
Light, Hugo Shelley.	Lieutenant.	68th Regiment.
Lilley, John.	Drummer 2702.	1st Scots Fus. Gds.
Lilley, John.	Quartermaster.	Grenadier Guards.
Lindsay, Henry Gore.	Captain.	Rifle Brigade.
Lindsell, Henry.	Gunner.	Royal Artillery.
Lindsell, R.H.	Major.	28th Regiment.
Llewellyn, R.	Captain.	46th Regiment.
Lock, S.	Corporal.	23rd Regiment.
Lodder, Henry Call.	Brevet Major.	47th Regiment.
Lovell, J. Williamson.	Captain.	Royal Engineers.
Lucan, G. C., Earl of.	Major General.	Staff; 8th Hussars.
Lunness, William.	Gunner/Driver.	Royal Artillery.
Lyle, Thomas.	Private.	42nd Regiment.
Lyons, [-].	Private.	21st Regiment.
Lyons, Timothy.	Private.	Royal Marines.

M'Donald, A. M'Ian.	Brevet Major.	Staff. (92nd Hdrs.)
M'Henry, J.	Lieutenant.	7th Regiment.
M'Neill, W.	Captain.	20th Regiment.
McArthur, Edward.	Lieutenant.	Royal Marines.
McClaming, John.	Private.	Royal Marines.
McCulloch, J.	Surgeon.	5th Dragoon Gds.
McDonald, Alexr.	Bombardier.	Royal Artillery.
McDonald, Alexr.	Private.	79th Regiment.
McDonald, Alexr.	Sergeant.	93rd Regiment.
McDonald, J.W.D.	Commander.	Royal Navy.
MacDonald, J.W.B.	Lieutenant Colonel.	Staff.
MacDonald, Michael.	Private.	8th Ryl. Irish Huss.
McElroy, John.	Private.	Royal Marines.
McEwen, John.	Sergeant.	79th Regiment.
McIntosh, Peter.	Bombardier.	Royal Artillery.
McKay, James.*	Private 4153.	1st Scots Fus. Gds.
McKay, John.	Private.	93rd Regiment.
McLagan, William.	Private.	1st Scots Fus. Gds.
MacLean, Fitzroy D.	Cornet.	13th Light Dragns.
MacNeill, Robert.	Lieutenant.	13th Light Dragns.
Madden, Daniel.	Corporal.	97th Regiment.
Madigan, T.	Private.	9th Regiment.
Magee, Thomas.	Corporal.	17th Lancers.
Maitland, C.L.B.	Lieutenant Colonel.	Grenadier Guards.
Maitland, K. Ramsay.	Captain.	79th Regiment.
Malone, Edward.	Corporal.	5th Dragoon Gds.
Maloney, Daniel.	Private.	44th Regiment.
Manson, John.	Private.	1st Regiment.
March, William Henry.	Captain.	Royal Marines.
Markham, Edwin.	Lieutenant.	Royal Artillery.
Marsh, Augustus L.	Captain.	55th Regiment.
Mason, William.	Leading Seaman.	Royal Navy.
Mason, William.	Colour Sergeant.	33rd Regiment.
Maude, G. Astley.	Major.	Royal Artillery.
Maxse, H.F.B.*	Captain.	1st Cold. Guards.
Maxwell, J. Pierce.	Brevet Lieut. Colonel.	50th Regiment.
Maycock, J. Gittens.	Captain.	14th Regiment.
Medlycott, Mervyn B.	Midshipman.	Royal Navy.
Melhuish, John.	Gunner.	Ryl. Marine Artilly.
Melson, Frederick.	Captain of the Aftguard.	Royal Navy.
Menzies, Duncan.	Private.	Scots Fus. Gds.
Meredith, H. Warter.	Captain.	41st Regiment.
Micklethwaite, G.	Captain.	44th Regiment.
Midgeley, William.	Private.	Royal Marines.

Milburn, S.	Private.	11th Hussars.
Miller, G. Murray.	Captain.	79th Regiment.
Mitchell, H.	Staff Surgeon.	
Mitford, Henry.	Lieutenant.	19th Regiment.
Molyneux, R.H.M.	Midshipman.	Royal Navy.
Moon, Thomas.	Private.	4th Light Dragns.
Mooney, J.	Leading Seaman.	Royal Navy.
Mooney, James.	Private.	7th Regiment.
Morant, Horatio H.	Captain.	68th Regiment.
Morgan, A.	Captain.	95th Regiment.
Morgan, G.C., the Hon.	Captain.	17th Lancers.
Morris, William.	Captain.	Royal Artillery.
Morrison, R. Fielding.	Captain.	19th Regiment.
Moulton, Charles.	Corporal 4392.	1st Scots Fus. Gds.
Mountain, Ephraim.	Private.	13th Light Dragns.
Muggridge, William.	Sergeant 3499.	Rifle Brigade.
Mullaney, Patrick.	Private.	95th Regiment.
Mullingar, [-].	Paymaster.	42nd Regiment.
Mulock, J.J.	Staff Surgeon.	
Mure, William.	Captain.	79th Regiment.
Murphy, Joseph.	Sergeant.	95th Regiment.
Naish, William.	Colour Sergeant.	Royal Artillery.
Nasmyth, Charles.	Major.	Staff. ([Ind. Army).
Neslon, M.H., the Hon.	Lieutenant.	Royal Navy.
Neville, [-].	Captain.	7th Regiment.
Newdigate, Edward.	Captain.	Rifle Brigade.
Newport, Simon G.	Captain.	39th Regiment.
Newton, Wm. Samuel.	Colonel.	1st Cold. Guards.
Nicholas, William.	Private.	1st Cold. Guards.
Nicolas, George T.	Mate.	Royal Navy.
Nicoll, Charles R.	Surgeon.	Grenadier Guards.
Nixon, A.	Captain.	89th Regiment.
Nixon, Arthur James.	Captain.	Rifle Brigade.
Noble, William	Private.	57th Regiment.
Noot, Edward Gregg.	Assistant Surgeon.	50th Regiment.
Norman, J.N.	Commander.	Royal Navy.
Nugent, Walter G.	Captain.	33rd Regiment.
O'Brien, J.	Captain.	30th Regiment.
O'Callaghan, John.	Private.	19th Regiment.
O'Connell, Denis.	Private 2494.	41st Regiment.
O'Donnel, Patrick.	Private.	1st Regiment.
O'Flynn, A.	Sergeant 1066.	88th Regiment.
Orlebar, O.	Captain.	28th Regiment.
Osborn, George.	Private.	Royal Marines.

Owen, B.	Corporal.	Grenadier Guards.
Owens, John.	Lieutenant.	33rd Regiment.
Owens, T.	Private.	23rd Regiment.
Owens, Thomas.	Colour Sergeant.	Royal Artillery.
Pain, S.	Sailmaker's Crew.	Royal Navy.
Pakenham, Thos. H.	Brevet Major.	30th Regiment.
Palmer, Thomas.	Private.	Rifle Brigade.
Parke, [-].	Private.	4th Dragoon Gds.
Parkinson, Charles.	2nd Master.	Royal Navy.
Paulet, G., Lord.	Captain.	Royal Navy.
Payne, Robert.	Leading Seaman.	Royal Navy
Paynter, David Wm.	Major.	Royal Artillery.
Pearce, George.	Leading Seaman.	Royal Navy.
Pengelley, E.	Leading Seaman.	Royal Navy.
Phelips, Henry P.P.	Captain.	Royal Artillery.
Philipps, J.L.	Captain.	89th Regiment.
Philips, N.G.	Captain.	47th Regiment.
Phillips, George.	Lieutenant.	Royal Engineers.
Phillips, John.	Sergeant Farrier.	Royal Artillery.
Poett, M.	Veterinary Surgeon.	1st Royal Dragns.
Ponton, [-].	Corporal.	4th Regiment.
Powell, T.	Lieutenant Colonel.	53rd Regiment.
Prendergast, Lenox.	Lieutenant.	2nd Dragoons.
Pressly, John.	Gunner/Driver.	Royal Artillery.
Prouse, William.	Sergeant 2077.	63rd Regiment.
Puget, Grenville Wm.	Captain.	34th Regiment.
Pye, John.	Private 1335.	1st Scots Fus. Gds.
Pym, Fredk. George.	Lieutenant.	Royal Marines.
Quail, Jessie.	Private.	4th Regiment.
Quinn, Hugh.	Private.	50th Regiment.
Quinn, Robert.	Private.	Royal Marines.
Radcliffe, Emil C. D.	Lieutenant.	88th Regiment.
Raffil, Peter.	Private.	1st Scots Fus. Gds.
Ravenhill, Philip.	Captain.	Royal Engineers.
Reedwood, Daniel.	Private 1837.	46th Regiment.
Reid, Patrick.	Private.	68th Regiment.
Reilley, Hugh.	Gunner/Driver.	Royal Artillery.
Reilly, John.	Cornet.	8th Ryl. Irish Huss.
Reynolds, R.C.	Engineer.	Royal Navy.
Richards, Edward.	Colour Sergeant.	Royal Marines.
Richards, W. Powell.	Captain.	Royal Artillery.
Richens, Elijah.	Private.	1st Scots Fus. Gds.
Ridley, Joseph.	Leading Seaman.	Royal Navy.
Ridley, William John.	Colonel.	1st Scots Fus. Gds.

Riley, John Edward.	Captain.	88th Regiment.
Roberts, J.L.	Sergeant.	1st Regiment.
Robertson, A.M.	Captain.	4th Dragoon Gds.
Robertson, William.	Private 4206.	1st Scots Fus. Gds.
Robinson, Andrew.	Gunner/Driver.	Royal Artillery.
Robinson, Charles.	Private.	Royal Marines.
Robinson, Robert.	Gunner/Driver.	Royal Artillery.
Robinson, Walter.*	Private.	1st Cold. Guards.
Robinson, William.	Private.	Royal Marines.
Rocke, Herbert.	Captain.	49th Regiment.
Rogers, H.D.	Captain.	Royal Navy.
Rogers, Henry.	Lieutenant.	Royal Navy.
Roggers, George.	Lance Corporal.	44th Regiment.
Rolinson, J.	Lieutenant.	Royal Navy.
Rolland, W.R.	Commander.	Royal Navy.
Rose, E.H.	Captain.	7th Regiment.
Rose, J.	Brevet Major.	30th Regiment.
Ross, John.	Captain.	Rifle Brigade.
Rourke, Michael.	Private.	6th Dragoons.
Rowan, Henry S.	Lieutenant Colonel.	Royal Artillery.
Rowe, J.*	2nd Captn. Foretop.	Royal Navy.
Rowles, James.	Captain.	Rifle Brigade.
Rudd, R.	Sergeant.	9th Regiment.
Russell, E., Lord.	Captain.	Royal Navy.
Rutter, John.	Private.	1st Cold. Guards.
Ryan, John.	Private 2644.	46th Regiment.
Saddler, Thomas.	Private.	8th Ryl. Irish Huss.
Sadler, James.	Private 1597.	47th Regiment.
Sankey, W.	Brevet Major.	47th Regiment.
Sarjent, Thomas.	Sergeant.	7th Regiment.
Saunders, T.M.	Surgeon on Staff.	Deputy Insp. Genl.
Sayer, Frederic.	Captain.	23rd Regiment.
Scarlett, J. York, Sir.	Major General.	Staff; 5th D. Gds.
Scholefield, [-].	Corporal.	4th Dragoon Gds.
Schooling, James.	Private.	Royal Marines.
Scott, John James.	Assistant Surgeon.	57th Regiment.
Scrutton, William.	Private.	1st Cold. Guards.
Sergent, Henry.	Private.	97th Regiment.
Seymour, W.H.	Captain.	68th Regiment.
Shakespear, G.B.	Major.	Royal Artillery.
Shawe, J.	Private.	23rd Regiment.
Sheldrake, Fredk.	Private.	1st Cold. Guards.
Shields, Alexander.	Sergeant Major.	6th Dragoons.
Shuckburgh, G.T.F.	Major.	1st Scots Fus. Gds.

23

Silver, Henry.	Gunner/Driver.	Royal Artillery.
Silver, Thomas R.	Cornet.	11th Hussars.
Simmons, John.	Private.	1st Cold. Guards.
Simpson, William.	Private.	4th Light Dragns.
Sinclair, William.	Assistant Surgeon.	93rd Regiment.
Siree, C.M.	Lieutenant.	33rd Regiment.
Skelton, [-].	Surgeon.	1st Cold. Guards.
Skelton, William.	Sergeant.	Royal Artillery.
Smith, Charles F.	Captain.	71st Regiment.
Smith, Charles.	Leading Seaman.	Royal Navy.
Smith, Edmund D.	Lieutenant	95th Regiment.
Smith, Edward.	Colour Sergeant.	Royal Marines.
Smith, H.	Corporal.	57th Regiment.
Smith, H.	Private.	9th Regiment.
Smith, M.	Corporal.	20th Regiment.
Smith, Samuel.	Gunner.	Ryl. Marine Artilly.
Southgate, Robert.	Sergeant Major.	77th Regiment.
Spooner, William	Sergeant 1262.	46th Regiment.
Stantiford, John.	Private.	Royal Marines.
Starling, J.	Boatswain.	Royal Navy.
Stevens, R.	Lieutenant.	21st Regiment.
Stewart, R.	Captain.	41st Regiment.
Stewart, W.R.	Assistant Surgeon.	Staff Surgeon.
Stirling, W.	Midshipman.	Royal Navy.
Stirrey, Charles.	Private.	1st Scots Fus. Gds.
Stoakes, James.	Private.	20th Regiment.
Stockwell, C.	Private.	7th Dragoon Gds.
Stokes, Oliver Haldam.	Lieutenant.	Royal Engineers.
Stone, James.	Colour Sergeant.	38th Regiment.
Stone, James.	Private.	38th Regiment.
Storer, T.W.	Captain.	68th Regiment.
Straton, R.J.	Lieutenant Colonel.	77th Regiment.
Stratton, Healey.	Private.	4th Light Dragns.
Streatfield, E.	Captain.	44th Regiment.
Sturt, Charles Napier.	Captain.	Grenadier Guards.
Such, Thomas.	Private.	42nd Regiment.
Sullivan, F.	Lieutenant.	Royal Navy.
Sutherland, F.	Captain.	2nd Dragoons.
Sutters, Joseph.	Private.	Royal Marines.
Sutton, Henry.	Gunner/Driver.	Royal Artillery.
Swinburne, John.	Captain.	18th Regiment.
Swinfen, Fredk. Hay.*	Captain.	5th Dragoon Gds.
Sykes, H.	Captain.	1st Royal Dragns.
Talbot, [-].	Private.	21st Regiment.

Talbot, William.	Sergeant.	1st Cold. Guards.
Talbott, A.	Sergeant Major.	1st Cold. Guards.
Taswell, Edward.	Captain.	Royal Artillery.
Taylor, Charles.	Private.	97th Regiment.
Taylor, G.	Lieutenant.	Royal Navy.
Taylor, John.	Sergeant.	30th Regiment.
Taylor, R.C. Hays.	Lieutenant Colonel.	79th Regiment.
Thomas, Elijah.	Corporal.	41st Regiment.
Thompson, Alexr.	Gunner/Driver.	Royal Artillery.
Thompson (Tompson), J.	Private.	90th Regiment.
Thompson, Thomas.	Lieutenant.	19th Regiment.
Thorne, Thomas.	Gunner's Mate.	Royal Navy.
Tibbs, Edward.	Gunner.	Ryl. Marine Artilly.
Tipping, Alfred.	Major.	Grenadier Guards.
Titcombe, John.	Private.	Rifle Brigade.
Toomey, Michael.	Able Seaman.	Royal Navy.
Torrens, A.W., Sir.	Brigadier General.	Staff.
Trevelyan, Harington A.	Captain.	11th Hussars.
Trevor, Fredk. Anthony.	Captain.	4th Regiment.
Trollope, Clifton.	Corporal.	Royal Artillery.
Troubridge, T.St.V.H.C.	Lieutenant Colonel.	7th Regiment.
Truston, Martin.	Private 2259.	41st Regiment.
Tryon, Thomas.	Captain.	7th Regiment.
Tucker, Jervis.	Lieutenant.	Royal Artillery.
Tulloch, Thomas.	Lieutenant Colonel.	42nd Regiment.
Turner, Alexander.	Private.	2nd Dragoons.
Turner, Henry Austin.	Major.	Royal Artillery.
Twamley, Thomas.	Private.	8th Ryl. Irish Huss.
Twysden, E. Fortescue.	Lieutenant.	55th Regiment.
Tyrwhitt, C.	Lieutenant Colonel.	1st Scots Fus. Gds.
Unett, Alexr. Fraser.	Lieutenant.	19th Regiment.
Unett, Thomas.	Lieutenant Colonel.	19th Regiment.
Upton, G., the Hon.	Colonel.	1st Cold. Guards.
Usher, Edward Price.	Captain.	Royal Marines.
Vernon, Henry Arthur.	Captain.	Royal Artillery.
Vesey, Arthur George.	Major.	46th Regiment.
Wakefield, H. Brevet	Major.	28th Regiment.
Waldy, Alfred Henry.	Captain.	46th Regiment.
Waldy, Wm. Thomas.	Lieutenant.	46th Regiment.
Walker, Charles P.B.	Major.	Staff. (2nd D. Gds.)
Walker, W.	Private.	11th Hussars.
Wallace, William.	Corporal.	Royal Artillery.
Walsh, Michael.	Corporal.	30th Regiment.
Walsh, Richard.	Private.	30th Regiment.

Walters, William	Private.	1st Scots Fus. Gds.
Walton, Francis.	Lieutenant.	Royal Marines.
Warenby, William	Private.	Royal Marines.
Warren, Arthur Fredk.	Captain.	Rifle Brigade.
Warren, Charles.	Colonel.	55th Regiment.
Watson, Wm. Henry.*	Lieutenant.	Royal Artillery.
Watt, [-].	Surgeon.	63rd Regiment.
Watt, George.	Private.	1st Scots Fus. Gds.
Watts, George.	Private.	Royal Marines.
Watts, James.	Private.	6th Dragoons.
Waymouth, W.	Lieutenant.	Royal Navy.
Weare, Henry Edwin.	Major.	50th Regiment.
Webb, William.*	Private	*See Well, Wm.*
Well, William.	Private.	20th Regiment.
Welsman, Robert.	Lance Corporal 1350.	41st Regiment.
West, Charles.	Leading Seaman.	Royal Navy.
Weston, Edmond.	Corporal.	Royal Artillery.
Wheatley, John.	Captain.	42nd Regiment.
White, A.	Lieutenant.	6th Dragoons.
Whitten, Andrew.	Lieutenant.	46th Regiment.
Wilberforce, H.W.	Lieutenant.	Royal Navy.
Wild, William.	Private.	28th Regiment.
Wilkins, [-].	Private.	5th Dragoon Gds.
Wilkinson, Fredk. G.	Captain.	42nd Regiment.
Williams, Charles.	Lance Corporal.	47th Regiment.
Willis, James.	Leading Seaman.	Royal Navy.
Wilson, C.	Lieutenant Colonel.	1st Cold. Guards.
Wilson, Robert.	Private.	Royal Marines.
Wilson, W.	Captain.	39th Regiment.
Wilson, W.L.	Lieutenant.	Royal Navy.
Wingfield, M.	Midshipman.	Royal Navy.
Wombwell, G.O., Sir.	Lieutenant.	17th Lancers.
Woods, Robert.	Private.	Royal Marines.
Woodwards, Samuel.	Private.	1st Dragoons.
Woolley, Bernard.	Private.	Royal Marines.
Wrenn, Cornelius.*	Colour Sergeant.	50th Regiment.
Wyatt, James.	Private 1847.	1st Scots Fus. Gds.
Yates, Henry Peel.	Major.	Royal Artillery.
Yates, John.	Private.	17th Lancers.
Yellop, Charles.	Private.	77th Regiment.
Yelverton, W.C.*	Major.	Royal Artillery.
Young, George.	Private.	50th Regiment.
Younghusband, C.W.	Captain.	Royal Artillery.

Regimental List

Regimental List

The list of officers and men of the Army, the Marines and the Royal Navy who received their medal from the Queen, arranged by order of regiment or unit.

The Royal Horse Guards.

Leslie, Thomas. Lieutenant.
> Served on the Staff (q.v.) as orderly to Lord Raglan.

The 2nd (Queens') Dragoon Guards.

Walker, Charles Pyndar Beauchamp. Major.
> Served on the Staff (q.v.) : A.D.C. to Lord Lucan.

The 4th (Royal Irish) Dragoon Guards.

Robertson, Arthur Masterson. Captain.
> Returned home in November, 1854 on Medical Certificate.
> Balaklava, Inkermann, Sebastopol : Turkish Crimea.

Gunter, Robert. Lieutenant.
> Returned home in October, 1854. Rejoined Regiment on the Bosphorus.
> Sebastopol : Turkish Crimea.

Innis, [-]. Farrier.
Parke, [-]. Private.
Scholefield, [-]. Corporal.
> Wounded.

The 5th (Princess Charlotte of Wales') Dragoon Guards.

Elliott, Alexander James Hardy. Captain.
> A.D.C. to Sir J.Y. Scarlett, with whom he returned home on 1st April, 1855. Wounded at Balaklava.
> Balaklava, Sebastopol : Knight, Legion of Honour : Turkish Crimea : Dispatches.

Swinfen, Frederick Hay. Captain.
> Returned home in November, 1854 on Medical Certificate. Wounded
> at Balaklava.
> Balaklava, Sebastopol : Turkish Crimea.

McCulloch, J. Surgeon.
> Returned home on 29th November, 1854 on Medical Certificate.

Carnay, [-]. Private.

Malone, Edward. Corporal.
> Wounded at Balaklava.

Wilkins, [-]. Private.

The 7th (Princess Royal's) Dragoon Guards.

Stockwell, C. Private.

The 1st (Royal) Dragoons.

Elmsall, William de Cardonnel. Captain.
> Returned home in October, 1854 : severely wounded at Balaklava.
> Balaklava, Sebastopol : Turkish Crimea : French Legion of Honour :
> Brevet Major.

Sykes, H. Captain.
> Returned home in October, 1854 on Medical Certificate.

Cruse, George. Lieut. (Riding Master).
> Balaklava, Inkermann, Sebastopol : Turkish Crimea.

Hartopp, William Wray. Lieutenant.
> Returned home in October, 1854 : wounded in the leg at Balaklava.
> Balaklava, Sebastopol : Turkish Crimea.

Poett, Matthew. Veterinary Surgeon.
> Returned home on 8th January, 1855 on Medical Certificate.
> Balaklava, Sebastopol : Turkish Crimea.

Woodwards, Samuel. Private.
> Wounded.

The 2nd (Royal North British) Dragoons.

Sutherland, F. Captain.
> Returned home in February, 1856; left the regiment.

Prendergast, Lenox. Lieutenant.
> Returned home in October, 1854 on account of wounds : severely
> wounded in left foot at Balaklava.
> Alma, Balaklava, Sebastopol : Turkish Crimea.

Adam, Charles. Private.
Hunter, Robert. Private.
Turner, Alexander. Private, 12541.
      Wounded.

The 4th (Queen's Own) Light Dragoons.

Ellis, George. Captain.
      Returned home on 26th October 1854 on Medical Certificate.
      Alma, Sebastopol : Turkish Crimea.

Hutton, Thomas. Captain.
      Sent to Scutari, October 1854 : gunshot wounds to left & right thigh,
      Balaklava. Retired 6th June, 1856.
      Alma, Balaklava, Sebastopol : Turkish Crimea.

Gore-Booth, Robert Newcomen. Lieutenant.
      Returned home in October, 1854 on Medical Certificate.
      Alma, Sebastopol : Turkish Crimea.

Crichton, Robert Orr. Assistant Surgeon.
      Returned home on 13th January, 1855 on Medical Certificate
      Alma, Inkermann, Balaklava, Sebastopol : Turkish Crimea.

Gillam, David J. Sergeant, 1130.
      Wounded at Inkermann.
      Distinguished Conduct Medal : Alma, Inkermann, Balaklava,
      Sebastopol : Knight, Legion of Honour : Turkish Crimea.

Moon, J. Thomas. Private.
      Sent home in March, 1855 : Wounded.
      Alma, Inkermann, Sebastopol : Turkish Crimea.

Simpson, William. Private.
      Sent home on 25th December, 1854.
      Alma : Turkish Crimea.

Stratton, Healey. Private.
      Groom to Capt. Hutton. Sent to Scutari, 1st October, 1854, "sick".
      Alma, Sebastopol : Turkish Crimea.

The 6th (Inniskilling) Dragoons.

White, A. Lieutenant.

Anderson, T.E. Lieut. (Riding Master).
      Attached to 13th Hussars.
      Alma, Balaklava, Sebastopol : Turkish Crimea.

Brown, John. Private.
Rourke, Michael. Private.
> Wounded at Balaklava.

Shields, Alexander. Sergeant Major.
> Wounded at Balaklava.

Watts, James. Private.
> Wounded.

The 8th (Royal Irish) Hussars.

Reilly, John. Cornet.
> Served with the 4th Dragoon Guards. Promoted from Regimental
> Sergt. Major. Rode in the Charge of the Heavy Brigade – horse
> wounded 3 times.
> Alma, Balaklava, Inkermann, Sebastopol : Turkish Crimea.

MacDonald, Michael. Private.
> Sent to Scutari, 26th October, 1854.
> Alma, Sebastopol : Turkish Crimea.

Saddler, Thomas. Private.
> Alma, Sebastopol : Turkish Crimea.

Twamley, Thomas. Private. Also occurs as Twohey.
> Severely wounded in the Charge of the Light Brigade, Balaklava.
> Distinguished Conduct Medal : Alma, Balaklava, Sebastopol :
> Turkish Crimea.

The 11th (Prince Albert's Own) Hussars.

Dallas, H. [? sc. Thomas Yorke]. Captain.
> Arrived and left between 27th and 31st December, 1854; home on
> Medical Certificate.

Trevelyan, Harington Astley. Captain.
> Wounded in left leg in the Charge of the Light Brigade at Balaklava.
> Returned home on 1st January, 1855. To 8th and then 7th Hussars.
> Alma, Balaklava, Sebastopol : 5th Class Medjidie : Turkish Crimea.

Silver, Thomas R. Cornet.
> Sergeant, commissioned as Cornet, 5th November, 1854.
> Half Pay 10th November, 1856. Adjutant of the West Kent
> Yeomanry.
> Alma, Sebastopol : Turkish Crimea.

Breeze, John. Sergeant.
> Wounded at Inkermann, lost his right arm.
> Yeoman of the Guard, 1855.
> Distinguished Conduct Medal : Alma, Inkermann, Sebastopol :
> Turkish Crimea. Photograph of this man in Abbott.

32

Clarke, William. Corporal.
> Alma, Sebastopol : Turkish Crimea.

Kilvert, John Ashley. Corporal.
> Twice wounded in the Charge of the Light Brigade at Balaklava.
> To England, February, 1855. One of the last survivors of the Charge.
> Alma, Balaklava, Sebastopol : Turkish Crimea.

Milburne, S. Private.
> Wounded in the right arm during the Charge of the Light Brigade at
> Balaklava.
> Alma, Balaklava, Sebastopol : Turkish Crimea.

Walker, W. Private.
> Wounded in left shoulder during the Charge of the Light Brigade at
> Balaklava.
> Alma, Balaklava, Sebastopol : Turkish Crimea.

The 13th Light Dragoons.

King, Edward Raleigh. Lieutenant.
> Returned home in September, 1854, invalided.
> Alma : Turkish Crimea.

MacLean, Fitzroy Donald. Cornet.
> On the Sick List on 25th October, 1854 and did not take part in the
> Charge. Died in 1936, the last known survivor of the Light Brigade.
> Alma, Sebastopol : Turkish Crimea.

MacNeill, Robert. Lieutenant.
> Alma, Sebastopol : Turkish Crimea.

Greatrex, Thomas Price. Cornet.
> Balaklava, Inkermann, Sebastopol : Turkish Crimea.

Gibbons, Abraham. Private.
> Alma, Sebastopol : Turkish Crimea.

Keene, John. Private.
> Wounded by canister in right leg in the Charge of the Light Brigade
> at Balaklava.
> Distinguished Conduct Medal : Alma, Balaklava, Sebastopol :
> Turkish Crimea.

Mountain, Ephraim. Private.
> Sent home on 25th November, 1854 : sick.
> Medal with no clasps : Turkish Crimea.

The 17th Lancers.

Lawrenson, John. Colonel.
> Commanded the regiment. "Sick", 21st September, 1854 and went
> home on 23rd October, 1854 on Medical Certificate, returning in
> 1855.
> Alma, Sebastopol : Turkish Crimea : Sardinian War Medal : 4th
> Class Medjidie.

33

Hartopp, John William Cradock. Captain.
> Sent home on 30th October, 1854 on Medical Certificate.
> Alma, Sebastopol : Turkish Crimea.

Morgan, Godfrey Charles, the Hon. Captain.
> Alma, Balaklava, Inkermann, Sebastopol : Turkish Crimea.

Wombwell, George Orb, Sir (Bart.). Lieutenant.
> On the Staff of Lord Cardigan ; briefly taken prisoner during the
> Charge of the Light Brigade. Returned Home 3rd February, 1855 on
> Private Affairs. Retired May, 1855.
> Alma, Balaklava, Inkermann, Sebastopol : Turkish Crimea.

Dimmock, William. Corporal.
> Rode in the Charge of the Light Brigade. To Scutari 26th October,
> 1854 and to England 9th December, 1854, with Captain White, 17th
> Lancers, whom he had rescued at Balaklava.
> Alma, Balaklava, Sebastopol : Turkish Crimea.

Magee, Thomas. Corporal.
> Wounded in the left thigh by grapeshot in the the Charge of the Light
> Brigade at Balaklava
> Alma, Balaklava, Sebastopol : Turkish Crimea.

Yates, John. Private.
> Wounded in right hand during the Charge of the Light Brigade at
> Balaklava. To Scutari, 12th December, 1854 and to England,
> 22nd March, 1855.
> Alma, Balaklava, Inkermann, Sebastopol : Turkish Crimea.

Officers on the Staff.

Cambridge, H.R.H. the Duke of. Lieut. General;
Colonel of the Scots Fusilier Guards etc.
> Commanded the 1st Division.
> Alma, Balaklava, Inkermann, Sebastopol : Turkish Crimea.

Cardigan, James Thomas Brudenell, Earl of. Major General;
11th Hussars.
> Commanded the Light Cavalry Brigade; led the Charge of the Light
> Brigade at Balaklava.
> Alma, Balaklava, Inkermann, Sebastopol : K.C.B. : Commander,
> Legion of Honour : 2nd Class Medjidie : Turkish Crimea.

Carpenter, [-]. Captain.
> Not identified.

Clifton, Thomas Henry. Captain.
> Served as A.D.C. to the Duke of Cambridge. Wounded at
> Inkermann; returned home in November, 1854 because of wounds.
> Alma, Balaklava, Inkermann, Sebastopol : Turkish Crimea : 5th
> Class Medjidie.

Conolly, James. Captain.
> Deputy Assistant Adjutant General; Brigade Major with Heavy
> Cavalry Brigade.
> Balaklava, Sebastopol : Knight of the Legion of Honour : 5th Class
> Medjidie : Turkish Crimea.

Evans, de Lacy, Sir. Lieutenant General, G.C.B.
> Commanded 2nd Division; wounded at the Alma.
> Alma, Balaklava, Inkermann, Sebastopol : G.C.B. : Grand Officer,
> Legion of Honour : 1st Class Medjidie : Turkish Crimea.

Evelyn, [-]. Lieutenant Colonel.
> Served on the Staff of the Turkish Army.

Jeffreys, Edmund Richard. Lieutenant Colonel.
> Commanded the 88th Regiment at Inkermann, where he was
> wounded. Returned home on 5th February, 1855 to join Depot
> Battalion at Parkhurst.
> Alma, Inkermann, Sebastopol : 5th Class Medjidie : Turkish Crimea.

Kane, [-]. Major.
> East India Company Service.

Leslie, Thomas. Lieut.; Royal Horse Guards.
> Wounded at the Alma; was Orderly Officer to Lord Raglan.
> Alma : Turkish Crimea.

**Lucan, George Charles Bingham, Earl of. Major General;
8th Hussars.**
> Commanded the Cavalry Division in the Crimea.
> Wounded at Balaklava.
> Alma, Balaklava, Inkermann, Sebastopol : K.C.B. : Commander,
> Legion of Honour : 1st Class Medjidie : Turkish Crimea.

**M'Donald, Alistair M'Ian. Brevet Major;
92nd Highlanders.**
> Served on Staff as Extra A.D.C. to General Pennefather. Returned
> home 5th November, 1854 because of severe wounds received at the
> Alma and at Inkermann.
> Alma, Inkermann, Sebastopol : 5th Class Medjidie : Turkish Crimea.

MacDonald, James William Bosville, the Hon. Lieut Colonel.
> A.D.C. to the Duke of Cambridge; returned home in November,
> 1854 with the Duke.
> Alma, Balaklava, Inkermann, Sebastopol : C.B. : Knight of the
> Legion of Honour : 5th Class Medjidie : Turkish Crimea.

Nasmyth, Charles. Major, East India Company Service.
> A.D.C. to Sir J. Burgoyne and Assistant Quarter Master General.
> Returned home on 5th November, 1854 on Medical Certificate.
> Alma, Sebastopol : Turkish Crimea : Turkish Gold Medal.

35

Scarlett, James Yorke, the Hon. Sir. Major General;
5th Dragoon Guards.
> Commanded the Heavy Cavalry Brigade in the Crimea.
> Alma, Balaklava, Inkermann, Sebastopol : K.C.B. : Commander,
> Legion of Honour : 2nd Class Medjidie : Sardinian War Medal :
> Turkish Crimea.

Torrens, A.W. , Sir. Brigadier General, K.C.B.
> Commanded the 2nd Brigade of the 4th Division at Inkermann ;
> wounded. Served from 14th September to 8th November, 1854 ;
> returned home sick on Medical Certificate.

Walker, Charles Pyndar Beauchamp. Major; 2nd Dragoon Guards.
> A.D.C. to Lord Lucan; returned home in November, 1854. Served on
> *Bellerophon* as a Volunteer during the bombardment of Sebastopol.
> Alma, Balaklava, Inkermann, Sebastopol : Turkish Crimea.

The Royal Engineers.

Gibb, Charles John. Captain.
> Sebastopol : 5th Class Medjidie : Turkish Crimea.

Lovell, John Williamson. Captain.
> Returned home on 6th November, 1854 on Medical Certificate.
> Alma, Sebastopol : 5th Class Medjidie : Turkish Crimea :
> Brevet Major.

Ravenhill, Philip. Captain.
> Returned home, invalided, in December, 1854.
> Alma, Inkermann, Sebastopol : 5th Class Medjidie : Turkish Crimea.

Lempriere, George Reid. Lieutenant.
> Returned home, invalided, in November, 1854. Also served with
> Turkish forces under Selim Pasha in 1854.
> Inkermann, Sebastopol : Turkish Crimea.

Phillips, George. Lieutenant.
> Returned home, invalided, in February, 1855.
> Alma, Inkermann, Sebastopol : 5th Class Medjidie : Turkish Crimea.

Stokes, Oliver Haldane. Lieutenant.
> Returned home, invalided, in March, 1855.
> Sebastopol : Turkish Crimea.

Medical Staff.

D'Arcey, O'Connor, M.D. Staff Surgeon.
> Returned home on 18th February, 1855 on Medical Certificate.
> Sebastopol : Turkish Crimea.

Dumbreck, David, M.D. Medical Staff.
>Senior Deputy Inspector General of Hospitals. In 1854, on "Special Service" – toured expected seat of war and reported. Returned home on 13th November, 1854 on Medical Certificate.
>Alma, Balaklava, Inkermann, Sebastopol : C.B. : 4th Class Medjidie : Turkish Crimea.

Ewing, J. Surgeon on the Staff.
>Deputy Inspector General.

Forrest, John. Doctor. Medical Staff.
>Deputy Inspector General of Hospitals. Returned home on 26th January, 1855 on Medical Certificate.
>Alma, Inkermann, Sebastopol : C.B. : 4th Class Medjidie : Turkish Crimea.
>Hon. Physician to the Queen : Mentioned in Dispatches for Inkermann.

Mitchell, H. Staff Surgeon.
>Returned home on 28th February, 1855.

Mulock, John Joseph. Staff Surgeon.
>Returned home on 16th February, 1855 on Medical Certificate.

Sunter, T.Moore, M.D. Surgeon on the Staff.
>Deputy Inspector General.
>Sebastopol : Turkish Crimea.

Stewart, W.R. Assistant Surgeon. Staff Surgeon.
>Returned home on 18th February, 1855 on Medical Certificate.

Commissariat Clerks.

Le Maitre, A. Acting Commissariat Clerk.
>Returned home on 16th February, 1855 on Medical Certificate.

Brown, [-]. Acting Commissariat Clerk.
>Not identified.

Chaplains.

Halpin, Robert, the Reverend. Chaplain.
>Sebastopol : Turkish Crimea.

The Royal Artillery.

Freese, John Noble Arbuthnot. Lieutenant Colonel.
>Returned home in February, 1855.
>Inkermann, Sebastopol : C.B. : 5th Class Medjidie : Turkish Crimea.

Gambier, Gloucester. Lieutenant Colonel.
>Invalided home in November, 1854.
>Inkermann, Sebastopol : C.B. : 5th Class Medjidie : Turkish Crimea.

Gilborne, Edward. Assistant Surgeon.
>Alma, Balaklava, Sebastopol : Knight, Legion of Honour : 5th Class
>Medjidie : Turkish Crimea.

Irving, Alexander. Lieutenant Colonel.
>Invalided home in March, 1855.
>Inkermann, Sebastopol : C.B. : 5th Class Medjidie : Turkish Crimea.

Lake, Noel Thomas. Lieutenant Colonel.
>Invalided home in December, 1854.
>Alma, Balaklava, Inkermann, Sebastopol : Legion of Honour : 5th
>Class Medjidie : Turkish Crimea.

Rowan, Henry Sebastian. Lieutenant Colonel.
>Returned home January, 1855.
>Inkermann, Sebastopol : C.B. : 5th Class Medjidie : Turkish Crimea.

Baddeley, J.F.Lodington.   Major.
>Wounded at Inkermann.
>Alma, Balaklava, Inkermann, Sebastopol : Legion of Honour : 5th
>Class Medjidie : Turkish Crimea.

Barstow, George. Major.
>Alma, Balaklava, Inkermann, Sebastopol : 5th Class Medjidie :
>Turkish Crimea.

D'Aguilar, Charles Lawrence. Major.
>Returned home in March, 1855; appointed to Royal Horse Artillery.
>Inkermann, Sebastopol : C.B. : 5th Class Medjidie : Turkish Crimea.

Franklin, Charles Trigance. Major.
>Invalided home in September, 1854.
>Alma, Sebastopol : C.B. : 5th Class Medjidie : Turkish Crimea.

Maude, George Astley. Major.
>Invalided home because of wounds in December, 1854.
>Alma, Balaklava, Sebastopol : C.B. : 5th Class Medjidie :
>Turkish Crimea.

Paynter, David William. Major.
>Invalided home in November, 1855.
>Alma, Balaklava, Inkermann, Sebastopol : C.B. : 5th Class Medjidie :
>Turkish Crimea.

Shakespear, George Bucknall. Major.
>Alma, Balaklava, Inkermann, Sebastopol : 5th Class Medjidie :
>Turkish Crimea.

Turner, Henry Austin. Major.
>[There seems to be no recorded Crimean War service for this
>officer.]

Yates, Henry Peel. Major.
>Invalided home December, 1854.
>Alma, Inkermann, Sebastopol : Sardinian War Medal : 5th Class
>Medjidie : Turkish Crimea.
>Brevet Major : Brevet Lieutenant Colonel.

Yelverton, William C., the Hon. Major.
>Inkermann, Sebastopol : 5th Class Medjidie : Turkish Crimea.

Bredin, Edgar Grantham. Captain.
>Returned home in March, 1855.
>Inkermann, Sebastopol : 4th Class Medjidie : Turkish Crimea :
>Brevet Major.
>Order of Medjidie for services with Osmanli Horse Artillery.

Brendon, Algernon. Captain.
>Returned home in March, 1855.
>Alma, Inkermann, Sebastopol : 5th Class Medjidie : Turkish Crimea.

Dashwood, Henry Walpole. J. Captain.
>Returned home in March, 1855.
>Alma, Balaklava, Inkermann, Sebastopol : Turkish Crimea.

De Havilland, James. Captain.
>Alma, Balaklava, Sebastopol : Turkish Crimea : Brevet Major.

Fraser, George Henry John Alexander. Captain.
>[There seems to be no recorded Crimean War service for this
>officer.]

Morris, William. Captain.
>Invalided home in December, 1854.
>Balaklava, Inkermann, Sebastopol : 5th Class Medjidie :
>Turkish Crimea.

Phelips, Henry Plantagenet Prescott. Captain.
>Alma, Sebastopol : Turkish Crimea.

Richards, W. Powell. Captain.
>Returned home in March, 1855.
>Alma, Balaklava, Inkermann, Sebastopol : Knight, Legion of Honour :
>Turkish Crimea.

Taswell, Edward. Captain.
>Invalided home, November, 1854.
>Inkermann, Sebastopol : Turkish Crimea.

Vernon, Henry Arthur. Captain.
>Sebastopol : Turkish Crimea.

Younghusband, Charles Wright. Captain.
>Inkermann, Sebastopol : Turkish Crimea.

Markham, Edwin. Lieutenant.
>Returned home in January, 1855; appointed to Royal Horse Artillery.
>Alma, Inkermann, Sebastopol : Knight, Legion of Honour : Turkish
>Crimea.

Tucker, Jervis. Lieutenant.
> Sebastopol : Turkish Crimea.

Watson, William Henry. Lieutenant.
> Invalided home in February, 1855.
> Inkermann, Sebastopol : Turkish Crimea.

Bagshaw, James. Gunner/Driver.
> Wounded at Inkermann.

Barfelt, Thomas. Sergeant.

Billington, Thomas. Gunner/Driver.

Boot, John E. Gunner/Driver.

Brown, William. Quartermaster Sergeant.

Bush, Henry. Gunner/Driver.

Carthew, George. Staff Wheeler.

Coachman, William. Driver.

Coy, Robert. Bombardier.

Crawford, William. Sergeant.
> Wounded at Inkermann. 4th Company, 12th Battalion.

Crowe, William. Sergeant.
> Wounded at Inkermann. 4th Company, 12th Battalion.

Davis, John. Gunner/Driver.

Dixon, William. Gunner/Driver.

Elliott, Henry. Bombardier.

Findley, David. Driver.

Gibbs, George. Gunner/Driver.

Goodman, James. Gunner/Driver.

Hains, John. Sergeant Major.

Hawkins, Robert. Bombardier.
> Wounded at Inkermann. 8th Company, 3rd Battalion.

Holmes, Joseph. Gunner/Driver.

Hooper, John. Sergeant.

Hughes, Charles. Gunner/Driver.
> Wounded in the trenches before Sebastopol.

Lindsell, Henry. Gunner.
> D.C.M. winner ; photograph in Abbott.

Lunness, William. Gunner/Driver.

McDonald, Alexander. Bombardier.
> Wounded in the trenches before Sebastopol.

McIntosh, Peter. Bombardier.

Naish, William. Colour Sergeant.

Owens, Thomas. Colour Sergeant.

Phillips, John. Sergeant Farrier.

Pressly, John. Gunner/Driver.
> Wounded in the trenches before Sebastopol.

Reilley, Hugh. Gunner/Driver.

Robinson, Andrew. Gunner/Driver.
> Wounded at the Alma.

Robinson, Robert. Gunner/Driver.
> Wounded at Inkermann. 8th Company, 3rd Battalion.
> D.C.M. winner ; photograph in Abbott.

Silver, Henry. Gunner/Driver.
Skelton, William. Sergeant.
Sutton, Henry. Gunner/Driver.
Thompson, Alexander. Gunner/Driver.
Trollope, Clifton. Corporal.
Wallace, William. Corporal.
Weston, Edmond. Corporal.

The Grenadier Guards.

Bradford, Ralph. Lieutenant Colonel.
> Wounded at Inkermann.
> Alma, Balaklava, Inkermann, Sebastopol : 5th Class Medjidie :
> Turkish Crimea.

Maitland, Charles Lennox Brownlow. Lieutenant Colonel.
> D.A.A.G., 4th Division. Severely wounded at Inkermann and sent
> home on 11th November, 1854.
> Alma, Balaklava, Inkermann, Sebastopol : Knight, Legion of Honour :
> 5th Class Medjidie : Turkish Crimea.

Cameron, William Gordon. Major.
> Severely wounded in the trenches before Sebastopol, 20th October,
> 1854. Sent home on the 13th January, 1855 on Medical Certificate.
> Alma, Sebastopol : Knight, Legion of Honour : 5th Class Medjidie :
> Turkish Crimea.

De Horsey, William Henry Beaumont. Major.
> Sent home 13th January, 1855 on Medical Certificate.
> Alma, Sebastopol : 5th Class Medjidie : Turkish Crimea : Brevet
> Major.

Tipping, Alfred. Major.
> Severely wounded at Inkermann and sent home 13th January, 1855
> on Medical Certificate.
> Alma, Balaklava, Inkermann, Sebastopol : Knight, Legion of Honour :
> 5th Class Medjidie : Turkish Crimea.

Burgoyne, John Montagu, Sir. Captain.
> Wounded at the Alma.
> Alma : 5th Class Medjidie : Turkish Crimea.

Sturt, Charles Napier. Captain.
> Severely wounded at Inkermann; returned home on 1st December,
> 1854 to join 2nd Battalion.
> Alma, Balaklava, Inkermann, Sebastopol : Sardinian War Medal :
> 5th Class Medjidie : Turkish Crimea.

Lilley, John. Quartermaster.
> Returned home on 19th February, 1855 to join 1st Battalion.
> Alma, Balaklava, Sebastopol : Turkish Crimea.

Nicoll, Charles R. Surgeon.
> Sebastopol : Turkish Crimea.

Owen, B. Corporal.
> Awarded the Distinguished Conduct Medal. Photograph in Abbott.

The 1st Coldstream Guards.

Newton, William Samuel. Colonel.
> Returned home on 8th April, 1855 to join 2nd Battalion.
> Balaklava, Inkermann, Sebastopol : 5th Class Medjidie : Turkish
> Crimea.

Upton, George Frederick, the Hon. Colonel.
> Wounded at Inkermann and horse killed.
> Alma, Balaklava, Inkermann, Sebastopol : C.B. : Officer, Legion of
> Honour : 3rd Class Medjidie : Turkish Crimea.

Dunkellin, Ullick Canning, Lord. Lieutenant Colonel.
> Alma, Sebastopol : 5th Class Medjidie : Turkish Crimea.

Fitzroy, Augustus Charles Lennox, Lord. Lieutenant Colonel.
> Severely wounded at Inkermann; returned home 7th November, 1854.
> Balaklava, Inkermann, Sebastopol : Sardinian War Medal : 5th Class
> Medjidie : Turkish Crimea.

Wilson, Charles Townshend. Lieutenant Colonel.
> Returned home on 22nd November, 1854 on Medical Certificate.
> Alma, Balaklava, Inkermann, Sebastopol : Turkish Crimea.

Feilding, Percy Robert Basil, the Hon. Brevet Major.
> Brigade Major, Brigade of Guards, at the Alma; Staff of 1st Division
> at Balaklava and Inkermann. Severely wounded at Inkermann.
> Alma, Balaklava, Inkermann, Sebastopol : Knight, Legion of Honour :
> 5th Class Medjidie : Turkish Crimea.

Amherst, William Archer, the Hon. Captain.
> Wounded at Inkermann and returned home on 7th November, 1854.
> Balaklava, Inkermann, Sebastopol : Turkish Crimea.

Baring, Charles. Captain.
> Wounded at Alma - arm amputated; rejoined and served before
> Sebastopol.
> Alma, Sebastopol : Knight, Legion of Honour : 5th Class Medjidie :
> Turkish Crimea.

Bingham, George, Lord. Captain.
> A.D.C. to Lord Lucan.
> Alma, Balaklava, Inkermann, Sebastopol : Knight, Legion of Honour :
> 5th Class Medjidie : Turkish Crimea.

Boyle, William George, the Hon. Captain.
>A.D.C. to Sir De Lacy Evans.
>Alma, Balaklava, Inkermann, Sebastopol : 5th Class Medjidie :
>Turkish Crimea.

Fitzroy, George Robert. Captain.
>Served with the 41st Regiment; severely wounded at Inkermann.
>Alma, Inkermann, Sebastopol : Turkish Crimea.

Maxse, Henry FitzHardinge Berkeley. Captain.
>A.D.C. to Lord Cardigan ; rode in the Charge of the Light Brigade.
>Returned home on 28th November, 1854 on account of wounds.
>Alma, Balaklava, Sebastopol : 5th Class Medjidie : Turkish Crimea.

Skelton, Joseph, M.D. Surgeon.
>Alma, Balaklava, Inkermann, Sebastopol : Turkish Crimea.

Stirling, Walter. Ensign.
>Served in Crimean campaign as Midshipman, *Britannia* : see Royal
>Navy section.

Ashkettle, James. Private.

Austin, Thomas. Colour Sergeant.
>Wounded at Inkermann.

Barnard, Emanuel. Private.
>Wounded at Inkermann.

Bridges, Frederick. Corporal.
>Wounded at Inkermann.
>D.C.M. winner ; photograph in Abbott.

Burrell, William. Private.
>Wounded at Inkermann.

Burt, John. Private.
>Wounded at Inkermann.

Burtonwood, Peter. Private.
>Wounded at Inkermann.
>Listed as Charles, not Peter, in casualty list.

Clatworthy, William. Private.
>Wounded at the Alma.

Garrad, Thomas. Private.

Gould, Wyndham. Private.
>Wounded at Inkermann.

Hadley, James. Private.

Harvey, Robert. Sergeant.

Hawkins, Joseph. Private.
>Wounded at Inkermann.

Hibbard, Samuel. Private.

Hoy, John. Private.
>Wounded at Inkermann.

King, John. Private.
>Wounded at Inkermann.

Lacey, James. Private.
Nicholas, William. Private.
Wounded at the Alma.
Robinson, Walter. Private.
Rutter, John. Private.
Wounded at the Alma.
Scrutton, William. Private.
Wounded at the Alma.
Sheldrake, Frederick. Private.
Wounded at Inkermann.
Simmons, John. Private.
Talbot, William. Sergeant.
Talbott, A. Sergeant Major.
Wounded at Inkermann.

The Scots Fusilier Guards.

Berkeley, Charles Ashton Fitzhardinge. Lieutenant Colonel.
Wounded at the Alma and returned home in September, 1854 on account of wounds.
Alma : Turkish Crimea.
Dalrymple, John Hamilton Elphinstone. Lieutenant Colonel.
Wounded at the Alma.
Alma, Inkermann, Sebastopol : 5th Class Medjidie : Turkish Crimea.
Ridley, William John. Colonel.
Returned to England on leave.
Alma, Balaklava, Inkermann, Sebastopol : 5th Class Medjidie : Turkish Crimea.
Tyrwhitt, Charles. Lieutenant Colonel.
A.D.C. to the Duke of Cambridge : returned home 3rd November, 1854.
Alma, Inkermann, Sebastopol : Knight, Legion of Honour : 5th Class Medjidie : Turkish Crimea.
Shuckburgh, George Thomas Francis. Major.
Wounded at Inkermann and returned home on account of wounds in November, 1854.
Alma, Balaklava, Inkermann : Turkish Crimea.
Damer, S. Captain.
Sent home sick in February, 1855.
Ennismore, Lord. Captain.
A.D.C. to Lt.General Wyndham. Became 3rd Earl of Listowel.
Wounded at the Alma and returned home in September, 1854 on account of wounds.

44

Fraser, Alexander Edward, the Hon. Captain.

> Alma, Balaklava, Inkermann, Sebastopol : Sardinian War Medal :
> 5th Class Medjidie : Turkish Crimea : Brevet Major.

Gipps, Reginald. Captain.

> Wounded at the Alma (bayonet) and at Inkermann. Returned home
> "sick" in November, 1854
> Alma, Balaklava, Inkermann, Sebastopol : Knight, Legion of Honour :
> 5th Class Medjidie : Turkish Crimea : Brevet Major.

Knollys, William Wallingford. Captain.

> Sebastopol : Turkish Crimea.

Annesley, Hugh, the Hon. Lieutenant.

> Severely wounded at the Alma and returned home on account of
> wounds in October, 1854.
> Alma, Sebastopol : Turkish Crimea.

Beaumont, Godfrey Wentworth. Lieutenant.

> Attached to the 21st Fusiliers.
> Alma, Balaklava, Inkermann, Sebastopol : Turkish Crimea.

Biddlecombe, George. Private.

> Wounded at the Alma.

Boyd, William. Private.

> Wounded at the Alma.

Bye, Richard. Sergeant.

> Wounded at the Alma.

Craw, John. Sergeant.

> Wounded at the Alma.

Drummond, Benjamin. Private 3718.

> Wounded at Inkermann.
> Balaklava, Inkermann, Sebastopol : Turkish Crimea.

Emery, Jonathan. Private 2594.

> Wounded at Inkermann.

Grimmond, Peter. Private.

Hannah, Alexander. Private.

> Wounded at the Alma and at Inkermann.

Joy, William. Private.

> Wounded at the Alma.

Juggins, William. Drummer 2912.

> Wounded at Inkermann.

Lilley, John. Drummer 2702.

> Wounded at Inkermann.

McKay, James. Private 4153.

> Wounded at Inkermann ; 2nd Battalion.

McLagan, William. Private.

> Wounded at the Alma.

Menzies, Duncan. Private.

Moulton, Charles. Corporal 4392.
>   Wounded at Inkermann.
>   D.C.M. winner ; photograph in Abbott.

Pye, John. Private 1335.
>   Wounded at Inkermann.

Raffil, Peter. Private.
>   Wounded at the Alma.

Richens, Elijah. Private.
>   Wounded at the Alma.

Robertson, William. Private 4206.
>   Wounded at Inkermann.

Stirrey, Charles. Private.

Walters, Thomas. Private.
>   Wounded at the Alma.

Watt, George. Private.
>   Wounded at the Alma.

Wyatt, James. Private 1847.
>   Wounded at Inkermann.

1st (Royal) Regiment.

Coles, Richard George. Captain.
>   Returned home on 5th February, 1855.
>   Alma, Inkermann, Sebastopol : Turkish Crimea.

Hearn, Charles Bush. Surgeon.
>   Returned home "sick" on 20th March, 1855.
>   Alma, Inkermann, Sebastopol : 5th Class Medjidie : Turkish Crimea.

Bevan, Samuel. Private.

Manson, John. Private.

O'Donnel, Patrick. Private.

Roberts, J. Lance Sergeant.

4th (King's Own) Regiment.

Trevor, Frederick Anthony. Captain.
>   Returned home on 16th February, 1855 to join Depot.
>   Alma, Inkermann, Sebastopol : Turkish Crimea.

Connally, John. Private. Also occurs as Connelly.

Dunn, Peter. Corporal.

Ponton, [-]. Lance Corporal.

Quail, Jessie. Private.

7th Regiment (Royal Fusiliers).

Troubridge, Thomas St.Vincent. H.C., Sir. Lieutenant Colonel.
>Severely wounded at Inkermann - both legs amputated; returned home in November, 1854.
>Alma, Inkermann, Sebastopol : 4th Class Medjidie : Turkish Crimea : A.D.C. :

Butler, H.W.P. Captain.
>Wounded at Inkermann and returned home on account of wounds in November, 1854.

Carpenter, George William Wallace. Captain.
>Wounded at the Alma and returned home in September, 1854 on Medical Certificate.
>Alma : Turkish Crimea.

Coney, Phillip George. Captain.
>Wounded at the Alma and returned home in September, 1854 on account of wounds.
>Alma : Turkish Crimea.

FitzGerald, W.H.D. Captain.
>Wounded at the Alma and returned home on account of wounds in September, 1854.
>Alma : Turkish Crimea.

Neville, [-]. Captain.

Rose, E.H. Captain.
>Wounded at Inkermann.

Tryon, Thomas. Captain.
>Returned home "sick" on 28th November, 1854.
>Inkermann, Sebastopol : Turkish Crimea.

Crofton, A., The Hon. Lieutenant.
>Served in the Crimea in September, 1854.

Disney, Edgar John. Lieutenant.
>Wounded and returned home "sick".

M'Henry, J. Lieutenant.
>Wounded before Sebastopol and returned home on account of wounds on 29th March, 1855.

Barrack, William. Private.
>Wounded at Inkermann.

Court, Thomas. Private.
>Wounded at the Alma.

Mooney, James. Private.
>Wounded at Inkermann.

Sarjent, Thomas. Sergeant.
>Wounded at Inkermann.

9th Regiment (East Norfolk).

Coyle, J. Private.
Madigan, T. Private.
Rudd, R. Sergeant.
Smith, H. Private.

14th Regiment (Buckinghamshire).

Maycock, John Gittens. Captain.
Served with the 47th Regiment. Wounded at the Alma and returned home on 12th February, 1855 to join Depot.
Alma, Inkermann, Sebastopol : Sardinian War Medal : 5th Class Medjidie : Turkish Crimea.

17th Regiment (Leicestershire).

Brinckman, T. Captain.
Served as Lieutenant in the Crimea from 17th December, 1854 to 7th February, 1855 ; to Depot.
Sebastopol : Turkish Crimea.
Earle, William Henry. Captain.
Sebastopol : Turkish Crimea.

18th Regiment (Royal Irish).

Swinburne, John. Captain.
Sebastopol : Turkish Crimea.

19th Regiment (1st Yorkshire North Riding).

Unett, Thomas. Lieutenant Colonel.
Mortally wounded in the assault on the Redan, 8th September, 1855. Buried in the cemetery of the 2nd Brigade, Light Division ; memorial stone.
Alma, Inkermann, Sebastopol : C.B. : Turkish Crimea : Dispatches.
Barrett, Richard Doyle. Captain.
Returned home on 8th February, 1855 on account of wounds but went back to the Crimea later.
Alma, Balaklava, Inkermann, Sebastopol : 5th Class Medjidie : Turkish Crimea.

48

Clay, George, Sir. (Bart.). Captain.
> Returned home on 19th February, 1855 on account of wounds.
> Alma, Inkermann, Sebastopol : 5th Class Medjidie : Turkish Crimea.

Jennings, George Bingham. Captain.
> Served in the Crimea from 7th October, 1854 to 29th December,
> 1854 and again from 17th October, 1855 to the end of the war.
> Sebastopol : Turkish Crimea.

Morrison, Richard Fielding. Captain.
> Returned home on 28th October, 1854 on Medical Certificate.
> Alma, Sebastopol : Turkish Crimea.

Currie, Leonard Douglas Hay. Captain.
> Wounded at the Alma and returned home on 28th October, 1854 on
> Medical Certificate.
> Alma : Turkish Crimea.
> Also served in the American Civil War in the 133rd New York
> Regiment ; wounded.

Mitford, Henry. Lieutenant.
> Inkermann, Sebastopol : Turkish Crimea.

Thompson, Thomas. Lieutenant.
> Carried the Colours at the Alma. Returned home on leave on 14th
> February, 1855.
> Alma, Inkermann, Sebastopol : Sardinian War Medal : Turkish
> Crimea.

Unett, Alexander Fraser. Lieutenant.
> Son of Lieut.Colonel Unett, 19th Regiment, q.v. Returned home on
> 28th October, 1854 on Medical Certificate.
> Sebastopol : Turkish Crimea.

Daly, Patrick. Sergeant.
> Wounded at the Alma.
> Alma : Turkish Crimea.

Edis, John. Private.
> Alma, Inkermann, Sebastopol : Turkish Crimea.

Hicks, Joseph. Private.
> Alma, Inkermann, Sebastopol : Turkish Crimea.

O'Callaghan, John. Private.
> Wounded.
> Alma, Inkermann : Turkish Crimea.

20th Regiment (East Devonshire).

Leet, E. Captain.
> Returned home on 22nd September, 1854 on Medical Certificate.

M'Neill, William Henry. Captain.
> Returned home in December, 1854 on Medical Certificate.
> Alma, Balaklava, Inkermann, Sebastopol : Turkish Crimea.

Adams, John M. Private 861.
>Wounded at Inkermann.

Smith, M. Corporal.

Stoakes, James. Private 2413.
>Wounded at Inkermann.

Webb, William. Private 1724. Also occurs as Well.
>Wounded at Inkermann. On roll as Webb.

21st Regiment (Royal North British Fusiliers).

Haines, Frederick Paul. Lieutenant Colonel.
>Alma, Balaklava, Inkermann, Sebastopol : 5th Class Medjidie :
>Turkish Crimea.

Boldero, George Neeld. Brevet Major.
>Wounded at Inkermann. Returned home in September, 1854 on
>Medical Certificate.
>Alma, Inkermann, Sebastopol : Sardinian War Medal : 5th Class
>Medjidie : Turkish Crimea : Brevet Major.

Stevens, R. Lieutenant.
>Wounded at Inkermann.
>Returned home in November, 1854 on account of wounds.

Bradshaw, [-]. Private.
>Wounded.

Lawson,   [-]. Corporal.

Lyons, [-]. Private.

Talbot, [-]. Private.

23rd Regiment (Royal Welsh Fusiliers).

Bathurst, Henry. Captain.
>Severely wounded at the Alma and returned home on 28th October,
>1854 on account of wounds.
>Alma : Turkish Crimea.

Bulwer, Edward Gascoigne. Captain.
>Returned home on 21st December, 1854 on Medical Certificate.
>Alma, Inkermann, Sebastopol : Turkish Crimea.

Granville, Bevil. Captain.
>Alma, Inkermann, Sebastopol : Turkish Crimea.

John, G. Captain.
>Returned home on 18th February, 1855 on Medical Certificate.

Sayer, Frederic. Captain.
>Severely wounded at the Alma and returned home on 28th October, 1854 on account of wounds
>Alma : Turkish Crimea.

Beechey, J. Private. Also occurs as Beachy.
>Wounded at the Alma.

Lock, S. Corporal.

Owens, T. Private.
>Wounded at the Alma.

Shawe, J. Private. Also occurs as Shave.
>Wounded at the Alma.

28th Regiment (North Gloucestershire).

Lindsell, Robert Henry. Major.
>Returned home on 15th February, 1855 - "Private Affairs".
>Alma, Inkermann, Sebastopol : 5th Class Medjidie : Turkish Crimea : Brevet Lt. Colonel.

Wakefield, Henry Furey. Brevet Major.
>Returned home on 12th November, 1854 on Medical Certificate.
>Alma, Sebastopol : Turkish Crimea.

Orlebar, O. Robert Hamond. Captain.
>Returned home on 20th February, 1854.
>Alma, Inkermann, Sebastopol : Knight, Legion of Honour : Turkish Crimea.

Carey, William. Private.

Edwards, John. Private.

Fitzgerald, Patrick. Private.

Wild, William. Private.

30th Regiment (Cambridgeshire).

Bayly, Paget. Brevet Major.
>Wounded at Sebastopol and Inkermann; returned home on account of wounds in November, 1854.
>Inkermann, Sebastopol : 5th Class Medjidie : Turkish Crimea.

Dickson, G. Brevet Major.
>Wounded at the Alma and Inkermann; returned home on account of wounds in September, 1854.
>Alma, Inkermann, Sebastopol : 5th Class Medjidie : Turkish Crimea.

Pakenham, Thomas Henry. Brevet Major.
>Wounded at the Alma; returned home on sick leave in October, 1854.
>Alma : Sardinian War Medal : 5th Class Medjidie : Turkish Crimea : Brevet Major.

Rose, James. Brevet Major.
> Wounded at Inkermann; returned home in October, 1854 on account of wounds.
> Alma, Inkermann, Sebastopol : 5th Class Medjidie : Turkish Crimea : Brevet Major.

Falkner, Edward Newstead. Captain.
> Served with Commissariat Department. Returned home on 22nd March, 1855 on Medical Certificate.
> Alma, Inkermann, Sebastopol : Turkish Crimea.

Harcourt, J. Captain.
> Returned home in September, 1854 on Medical Certificate.

O'Brien, John. Captain.
> Returned home in October, 1854 on sick leave.
> Alma : Turkish Crimea.

Fyffe, Wm. Johnstone, M.D. Assistant Surgeon.
> Returned home in November, 1854 on Medical Certificate.
> Alma, Inkermann, Sebastopol : Turkish Crimea.

Taylor, John. Sergeant.

Walsh, Michael. Corporal. Also occurs as Welsh.

Walsh, Richard. Private. Also occurs as Welsh.
> Wounded at the Alma.

33rd Regiment. (Duke of Wellington's).

Gough, T.B. Brevet Lieutenant Colonel.
> Wounded at the Alma : died of the effects of his wounds on 18th September, 1855. Buried in the cemetery of the 1st Brigade, Light Division.

Nugent, Walter George. Captain.
> Sent home as supernumerary, 5th February, 1855.
> Alma, Inkermann, Sebastopol : 5th Class Medjidie : Turkish Crimea.

Greenwood, John James. Lieutenant.
> Severely wounded whilst carrying the colours at the Alma.
> Returned home on 21st November, 1854 on account of wounds.
> Alma : Turkish Crimea.

Kenrick, Buxton Martin. Lieutenant.
> Returned home on 24th December, 1854 on Medical Certificate.
> Inkermann, Sebastopol : Turkish Crimea.

Owens, John. Lieutenant.
> Wounded at Inkermann and before Sebastopol. Returned home on 21st November, 1854 on account of wounds.
> Alma, Inkermann, Sebastopol : 5th Class Medjidie : Turkish Crimea.

Siree, Charles Moore B. Lieutenant.
> Severely wounded whilst carrying the colours at the Alma. Returned home on 21st November, 1854 on account of wounds.
> Alma : Turkish Crimea.

Burton, William. Private.
>Wounded at the Alma.

Crowley, Jeremiah. Private.
>Wounded at the Alma.

Gaffney, James. Private.
>Wounded at the Alma.

Keane, William. Sergeant.
>Wounded at the Alma.

Mason, William. Colour Sergeant.
>Wounded at the Alma.

34th Regiment (Cumberland).

Puget, Grenville William. Captain.
>Sebastopol : Turkish Crimea.

38th Regiment (1st Staffordshire).

Beswick, J. Captain.
>Returned home on 8th November, 1854 on leave.

Craster, James Thomas. Captain.
>Returned home on leave on 26th November, 1854.
>Alma, Inkermann, Sebastopol : Turkish Crimea.

Gloster, Edward T. Captain.
>Returned home on 23rd January, 1855 and went back to Crimea on
>29th August, 1855.
>Alma, Inkermann, Sebastopol : Turkish Crimea : Brevet Major.

Doherty, Daniel. Quartermaster.
>Returned home on 24th December, 1854 on Medical Certificate.
>Inkermann, Sebastopol : Turkish Crimea.

Goodall, William. Corporal.
>Wounded.

Kite, Isaac. Private.
>Wounded.

Stone, James. Colour Sergeant.
>Wounded.

Stone, James. Private.
>Wounded.

39th Regiment (Dorsetshire).

Agnew, James. Captain.
>Returned home on 16th February, 1855 to join the Depot.
>Sebastopol : Turkish Crimea.

Dixon, Thomas Fraser. Captain.
> Returned home on 8th February, 1855 to join the Depot.
> Sebastopol : Turkish Crimea.

Newport, Simon George. Captain.
> Sebastopol : Turkish Crimea.

Wilson, W. Captain.
> Returned home on 16th February, 1855 to join the Depot.
> Sebastopol : Turkish Crimea.

41st Regiment (Welsh).

Bligh, Frederick Cherburgh. Captain.
> Wounded at Inkermann. Returned home on 8th November, 1854 on Medical Certificate.
> Inkermann, Sebastopol : Turkish Crimea.

Bush, Henry Stratton. Captain.
> Wounded at Inkermann and returned home on 13th January, 1855 on Medical Certificate.
> Alma, Inkermann, Sebastopol : Sardinian War Medal : Turkish Crimea.

Meredith, Henry Warter. Captain.
> Wounded at Inkermann and returned home on 27th October, 1854 on account of wounds.
> Alma, Inkermann, Sebastopol : 5th Class Medjidie : Turkish Crimea : Brevet Major.

Steward, Robert Oliver Francis. Captain.
> Returned home on 19th October, 1854 on Medical Certificate.
> Alma, Sebastopol : 5th Class Medjidie : Turkish Crimea.

Abbott, Frederick Tydd. Assistant Surgeon.
> Returned home on 25th March, 1855 – "private affairs".
> Alma, Inkermann, Sebastopol : Turkish Crimea.

King, [-]. Assistant Surgeon.
[See also **Fitzroy, George Robert. Captain, Coldstream Guards.**]
O'Connell, Denis. Private 2494.
> Wounded at Inkermann.

Thomas, Elijah. Corporal.
Truston, Martin. Private 2259.
> Wounded at Inkermann.

Welsman, Robert. Lance Corporal 1350.
> Wounded at Inkermann.

42nd Regiment (Royal Highland).

Cameron, Alexander. Lieutenant Colonel.
>Alma, Balaklava, Sebastopol : Turkish Crimea : Sardinian War Medal.

Tulloch, Thomas. Lieutenant Colonel.
>Commanded the regiment. Returned home on 11th February, 1855 to join the Depot.
>Alma, Balaklava, Sebastopol : 5th Class Medjidie : Turkish Crimea.

Campbell, Archibald Colin. Brevet Major.
>Returned home on 21st November, 1854 on Medical Certificate.
>Alma, Balaklava : Sebastopol : Turkish Crimea.

Wheatley, John. Captain (Paymaster).
>Returned home in December, 1854 on Medical Certificate.
>Alma, Sebastopol : Turkish Crimea.

Wilkinson, Frederick Green. Captain.
>Returned home in March, 1855 to rejoin the Depot.
>Alma, Sebastopol : 5th Class Medjidie : Turkish Crimea.

Mullingar, [-]. Paymaster.
>Not identified in records.

Fox, George. Corporal.
>Severely wounded before Sebastopol, 18th to 21st October, 1854.
>Alma, Sebastopol : 5th Class Medjidie : Medaille Militaire : Turkish Crimea.

Lawson, David. Private. Forename also occurs as George.
>Wounded.
>Alma, Sebastopol : Turkish Crimea.

Lyle, Thomas. Private. Also occurs as Lyall.
>Wounded at the Alma.
>Alma : Turkish Crimea.

Such, Thomas. Private. Also occurs as Leitch.
>Wounded at the Alma.
>Alma : Turkish Crimea.

44th Regiment (East Essex).

Brown(e), Andrew. Brevet Lieutenant Colonel.
>Wounded at the Alma – lost his right arm and left hand. Returned home to Depot in December, 1854 on account of wounds.
>Alma, Sebastopol : Knight, Legion of Honour : 5th Class Medjidie : Turkish Crimea : Brevet Major and Brevet Lt. Colonel.

Micklethwaite, George N. Captain.
>Returned home to Depot on 2nd January, 1855 on sick leave.
>Alma, Inkermann, Sebastopol : Turkish Crimea.

Streatfield, E. Captain.
>Returned home on 20th October, 1854 on Medical Certificate.

Bradford, M. Lieutenant
>Returned home in December, 1854 on Medical Certificate.

Carney, William. Private.
>Wounded.

George, Henry. Private.
>Wounded.

Maloney, Daniel. Private.
>Wounded.

Roggers, George. Lance Corporal.
>Wounded.

46th Regiment (South Devonshire).

Vesey, Arthur George. Major.
>Returned home on 8th February, 1855 to join Depot.
>Sebastopol : 5th Class Medjidie : Turkish Crimea.

Fane, John Augustus. Captain.
>Returned home on 6th February, 1855 to join Depot.
>Sebastopol : Turkish Crimea.

Llewellyn, R. Captain.
>Wounded : returned home on account of wounds on 16th December,
>1854. Left the regiment on 6th March, 1855.

Waldy, Alfred Henry. Captain.
>Returned home on 6th February, 1855 to join Depot.
>Sebastopol : Turkish Crimea.

Waldy, William Thomas. Lieutenant.
>Sebastopol : Turkish Crimea.

Whitten, Andrew. Lieutenant.
>Returned home on 6th February, 1855 to join Depot.
>Sebastopol : Turkish Crimea.

Goss, James. Private 3201.
>Sent home 24th March, 1855.
>Alma, Inkermann, Balaklava, Sebastopol : Turkish Crimea.

Reedwood, Daniel. Private 1837.
>Alma, Inkermann, Sebastopol : Turkish Crimea.

Ryan, John. Private 2644.
>Returned home 14th March, 1855.
>Alma, Inkermann, Balaklava, Sebastopol : Turkish Crimea.

Spooner, William. Sergeant 1262.
>Sent home 24th March, 1855.
>Alma, Balaklava, Sebastopol : Turkish Crimea.

47th Regiment (Lancashire).

Haly, William O'Grady. Lieutenant Colonel.
Commanded 2nd Brigade of 2nd Division. Wounded at Inkermann –
4 bayonet wounds. Returned home in November, 1854 on account of
wounds.
Alma, Inkermann, Balaklava, Sebastopol : C.B. : Officer, Legion of
Honour : 3rd Class Medjidie : Turkish Crimea.

Lodder, Henry Call. Brevet Major.
Returned home on 1st November, 1854 on Medical Certificate.
Alma, Balaklava, Sebastopol : Turkish Crimea.

Sankey, William. Brevet Major.
Deputy Assistant (later Assistant) Quartermaster General, 1st
Division. Returned home on 1st November, 1854 on Medical
Certificate.
Alma, Balaklava, Sebastopol : 5th Class Medjidie : Turkish Crimea :
Brevet Major and Brevet Lt.Colonel.

Philips, Nathaniel George. Captain.
Wounded at the Alma. Returned home on 3rd January, 1855 to join
the Depot.
Alma, : Turkish Crimea.

Cross, Charles. Sergeant 1866.
Wounded at Inkermann.

Gallagher, Peter. Private.

Sadler, James. Private 1597.
Wounded at Inkermann.

Williams, Charles. Lance Corporal.
Wounded at the Alma.

49th Regiment (Hertfordshire).

Astley, Richard D. Captain.
Returned home 8th February, 1855; promoted.
Alma, Inkermann, Sebastopol : Turkish Crimea.

Corban, William Watts. Captain.
Returned home 25th February, 1855 to join Depot.
Alma, Inkermann, Sebastopol : Turkish Crimea.

Rocke, Herbert. Captain.
Returned home 12th November, 1854 and went back to the Crimea
on 3th October, 1855.
Alma, Inkermann, Sebastopol : Turkish Crimea.

Cahill, Patrick. Lieutenant
Carried the colours at the Alma : wounded. Returned home on
account of wounds in January, 1855.
Alma, Sebastopol : Turkish Crimea.

Coleman, Ryan. Private 2804.
Wounded at Inkermann.
Cross, Robert. Sergeant.
Cunningham, John. Corporal 3041.
Wounded at Inkermann.
Harin, Dinnes. [Dennis ?] Private.
Wounded.

50th Regiment (Queen's Own).

Maxwell, James Pierce, the Hon. Brevet Lieutenant Colonel.
Severely wounded in the head by a round shot before Sebastopol.
Returned home on account of wounds on 3rd November, 1854.
Alma, Sebastopol : 5th Class Medjidie : Turkish Crimea : Brevet
Lt.Colonel.
Weare, Henry Edwin. Major.
Assistant Quartermaster General. Wounded at the Alma and returned
home on account of wounds on 20th September, 1854.
Alma, Sebastopol : Sardinian War Medal : 5th Class Medjidie :
Turkish Crimea.
Noott, Edward Gregg. Assistant Surgeon.
Returned home sick on 16th November, 1854; back to Crimea on
7th July, 1855.
Alma, Inkermann, Sebastopol : Turkish Crimea.
Land, James. Private.
Quinn, Hugh. Private.
Wrenn, Cornelius. Colour Sergeant.
Alma, Sebastopol : Turkish Crimea.
Young, George. Private.

53rd Regiment (Shropshire).

Powell, Thomas Sydney. Lieutenant Colonel.
Served in command (and later as second-in-command) of the 57th
Regiment. Returned home in January, 1855.
Balaklava, Inkermann, Sebastopol : Turkish Crimea.

55th Regiment (Westmoreland).

Warren, Charles. Colonel, C.B.
Commanded the 55th at the Alma and 1st Brigade, 2nd Division at
Inkermann. Wounded at the Alma, twice wounded at Inkermann and
again before the Redan. Returned home in November, 1854 on
account of wounds.
Alma, Inkermann, Sebastopol : Sardinian War Medal : Officer,
Legion of Honour : 3rd Class Medjidie : Turkish Crimea.

Coats, John. Major.

> Wounded at the Alma : returned home in October, 1854 on account of wounds.
>
> Alma : Turkish Crimea.

Armstrong, Edward Marcus. Captain.

> Severely wounded at the Alma : returned home in October, 1854 on account of wounds.
>
> Alma : Turkish Crimea.

Barnston, William. Captain.

> Severely wounded at Inkermann; returned home to Depot on 16th January, 1855 on account of wounds.
>
> Alma, Inkermann, Sebastopol : Knight, Legion of Honour : Turkish Crimea.

Bissett, George Edward L.C. Captain.

> Wounded at the Alma; returned home on 28th October, 1854 on account of wounds.
>
> Alma, Sebastopol : Turkish Crimea.

Brown, Thomas Southwell. Captain.

> Returned home on 26th February, 1855 Medical Certificate.
>
> Alma, Inkermann, Sebastopol : 5th Class Medjidie : Turkish Crimea.

England, Richard. Captain.

> A.D.C. to General Sir R. England. Returned home on 18th November, 1854 on Medical Certificate.
>
> Inkermann, Sebastopol : 5th Class Medjidie : Turkish Crimea.

Hume, Robert. Captain.

> Wounded at Inkermann; returned home on 13th January, 1855 on account of wounds.
>
> Alma, Inkermann, Sebastopol : Knight, Legion of Honour : 5th Class Medjidie : Turkish Crimea.

Marsh, Augustus Leacock. Captain.

> Commanded the 55th at Inkermann; returned home on 21st November, 1854 on Medical Certificate.
>
> Alma, Inkermann, Sebastopol : Turkish Crimea.

Twysden, Edmond Fortescue. Lieutenant.

> Returned home sick on 6th November, 1854.
>
> Alma, Inkermann, Sebastopol : Turkish Crimea.

Farrel, John. Private.

> Wounded.

Foster, John. Private.

Fox, Edward. Private 1324.

> Wounded at Inkermann.

Hudson, Daniel. Private.

57th Regiment (West Middlesex).

Copeland, Alex Lester. Captain.
Returned home to Depot on 7th February, 1855.
Sebastopol : Turkish Crimea.

Buller, James Hornby. Lieutenant.
Returned home on 28th November, 1854 on Medical Certificate.
Sebastopol : Turkish Crimea.

Scott, John James. Assistant Surgeon.
Returned to England with invalids on 23rd March, 1855.
Balaklava, Inkermann, Sebastopol : Turkish Crimea.
"Mentioned" for gallantry under fire at Inkermann.
[See also **Lieutenant Colonel T. Powell, 53rd Regiment**].

Keeting, James. Corporal.
Wounded at Inkermann.

Noble, William. Private.
Wounded at Inkermann.

Smith, H. Corporal.

63rd Regiment (West Suffolk).

Dalzell, Robert Alex. George, the Hon. Lieutenant Colonel, C.B.
Returned home in April, 1855 on Medical Certificate.
Alma, Inkermann, Balaklava, Sebastopol : Sardinian War Medal :
Turkish Crimea.

Harries, Thomas. Major.
Wounded at Inkermann; returned home to depot, sick, in January,
1855.
Alma, Inkermann, Balaklava, Sebastopol : Knight, Legion of Honour :
5th Class Medjidie : Turkish Crimea.

Bamford, Robert Carter. Captain.
Returned home in January, 1855 on Medical Certificate.
Alma, Inkermann, Balaklava, Sebastopol : Turkish Crimea.

Cockburn, J. Captain.
Returned home in January, 1855 on Medical Certificate.

Fairtlough, Charles Edward. Captain.
Wounded at Inkermann; returned home in March, 1855.
Alma, Inkermann, Balaklava, Sebastopol : Sardinian War medal :
5th Class Medjidie : Turkish Crimea.

Johns, T. Captain.
Wounded at Inkermann; returned home in January, 1855 on Medical
Certificate.

Flower, W. Assistant Surgeon.
>Returned home in December, 1854 on Medical Certificate.

Watt, [-]. Surgeon.

Erwin, James. Private.

Gaffney, James. Private.

Hague, Dennis. Private.

Prouse, William. Sergeant 2077.
>Wounded at Inkermann.

68th Regiment (Durham).

Fitzroy, Cavendish C. Captain.
>Returned home to Depot on 7th February, 1855 on promotion.
>Alma, Inkermann, Sebastopol : 5th Class Medjidie : Turkish Crimea.

Morant, Horatio Harbord. Captain.
>A.D.C. to Brigadier General H. Shirley. Returned home to depot on 8th November, 1854 on Medical Certificate. Fractured right arm in trenches before Sebastopol.
>Alma, Inkermann, Sebastopol : Turkish Crimea.

Seymour, W.H. Captain.
>Returned home on 5th April, 1855 on "private affairs".

Storer, T.W. Captain. Initial also occurs as J.
>Returned home on 5th April, 1855 on Medical Certificate.

Cator, John. Lieutenant.
>Wounded at Inkermann; returned home on 8th November, 1854 on account of wounds.
>Alma, Inkermann, Sebastopol : Turkish Crimea.

Light, Hugo Shelley. Lieutenant.
>Returned home to depot, sick, on 23rd October, 1854.
>Alma, Sebastopol : Turkish Crimea.

Johnston, A. Assistant Surgeon.

Boden, John. Private.

Reid, Patrick. Private. Also occurs as Reed.
>Wounded.

71st Regiment (Highland Light Infantry).

Blenerhasset, Barry. Captain.
>Returned home to Depot on 13th February, 1855.
>Sebastopol : Turkish Crimea.

Smith, Charles Francis. Captain.
>Returned home on to Depot 13th February, 1855
>Sebastopol : Turkish Crimea.

77th Regiment (East Middlesex).

Straton, Robert Jocelyn. Lieutenant Colonel, C.B.
>   Returned home, sick.
>   Alma, Inkermann, Sebastopol : C.B. : Turkish Crimea : Brevet
>   Lt.Colonel.

Carden, Henry Robert. Captain.
>   Returned home to Depot on 15th December, 1854.
>   Alma, Inkermann, Sebastopol : Knight, Legion of Honour : 5th Class
>   Medjidie : Turkish Crimea.

Brown, Samuel. Private.

Cromwell, Matthew. Private.

Dillon, Charles. Corporal.
>   Wounded.

Southgate, Robert. Sergeant Major.

Yellop, Charles. Private.

79th Regiment (Cameron Highlanders).

Taylor, Richard Chambre Hays. Lieutenant Colonel.
>   Returned home on sick leave, 9th February, 1855; back to the
>   Crimea on 15th June.
>   Alma, Balaklava, Sebastopol : 5th Class Medjidie : Turkish Crimea.

Cuninghame, William Cuninghame. Captain.
>   Returned home on 26th November, 1854 on Medical Certificate.
>   Alma, Balaklava, Sebastopol : Turkish Crimea.

Freme, J. Captain.
>   Returned home to join Depot on 9th February, 1855.

Maitland, Keith Ramsay.   Captain.
>   Returned home to join Depot on 9th February, 1855.
>   Alma, Inkermann, Sebastopol : Turkish Crimea.

Miller, George Murray. Captain.
>   Returned home to join Depot on 16th January, 1855.
>   Alma, Balaklava, Sebastopol : Turkish Crimea.

Mure, William. Captain.
>   Returned home to join Depot on 9th February, 1855.
>   Alma, Balaklava, Sebastopol : Turkish Crimea.

Cornes, John. Paymaster.
>   Returned home on 21st December, 1854 on Medical Certificate.
>   Alma, Sebastopol : Turkish Crimea.

Anderson, James. Private.
>   Wounded at the Alma.

Borthwick, Charles. Private.
McDonald, Alexander. Private.
Wounded.
McEwen, John. Sergeant.

88th Regiment (Connaught Rangers).

Jeffreys, Edmund Richard. Lieutenant Colonel.
On Staff Roll but commanded the 88th Regiment at Inkermann, where he was wounded. Returned home on 5th February, 1855 to join Depot Battalion at Parkhurst.
Alma, Inkermann, Sebastopol : 5th Class Medjidie : Turkish Crimea.

Brown, Edward John Vesey. Major.
Returned home on 7th December, 1854 on sick leave.
Alma, Inkermann, Sebastopol : Sardinian War Medal : Turkish Crimea.

Baynes, H.J. Le Marchant. Captain.
Wounded at Inkermann and returned home in December, 1854 on account of wounds.
Alma, Inkermann, Sebastopol : Turkish Crimea.

Crosse, Joshua Grant. Captain.
Wounded at Inkermann and returned home in December, 1854 on Medical Certificate.
Alma, Inkermann, Sebastopol : Turkish Crimea.

Henning, Shurlock. Captain.
Returned home in November, 1854 on sick leave.
Alma, Sebastopol : Turkish Crimea.

Riley, John Edward. Captain.
Returned home on 1st January, 1855 on Medical Certificate.
Alma, Inkermann, Sebastopol : Sardinian War Medal : Turkish Crimea.

Radcliffe, Emil C. Delme. Lieutenant.
Returned home in November, 1854 on sick leave.
Alma, Sebastopol : Turkish Crimea.

O'Flynn, A. Sergeant 1066.
Wounded at Inkermann.

Day, Martin. Private.
Wounded at the Alma.

Kelly, Patrick. Private.
Wounded.

Killilea, Thomas. Private.
Wounded at the Alma.

89th Regiment.

Nixon, A. Captain.
> Returned home to join Depot on 16th February, 1855.
> Sebastopol : Turkish Crimea.

Philipps, John Lewes. Captain.
> Returned home to join Depot on 3rd (or 14th) February, 1855.
> Sebastopol : Turkish Crimea.

Cresswell, George. Lieutenant.
> Returned home on 15th February, 1855 on Medical Certificate.
> Sebastopol : Turkish Crimea.

90th Regiment (Perthshire Volunteers).

Guise, John Christopher. Captain.
> Returned home on 24th December, 1854 on Medical Certificate.
> Sebastopol : Turkish Crimea.

Irby, Leonard H. Lloyd. Lieutenant.
> Returned home on 20th March, 1855 on Medical Certificate.
> Sebastopol : Turkish Crimea.

Bull, John. Private.
Hall, John. Private.
Thompson (or Tompson), John. Private.

92nd Regiment (Gordon Highlanders).

M'Donald, Alistair M'Ian. Brevet Major.
> Served on Staff (q.v.) as Extra A.D.C. to General Pennefather.

93rd Regiment (Sutherland Highlanders).

Hay, Alex Sebastian Leith. Lieutenant Colonel, C.B.
> On leave from the Crimea between 8th February and 13th August, 1855.
> Alma, Balaklava, Sebastopol : Knight, Legion of Honour : 5th Class Medjidie : Turkish Crimea.

Dawson, E.S. Francis George. Captain.
> Arrived on 14th September, 1854 and returned home on 8th February, 1855 to join Depot.
> Alma, Balaklava, Sebastopol : Turkish Crimea.

Clayhills, James Menzies. Lieutenant.
> Returned home on 14th July, 1855 on Medical Certificate.
> Balaklava, Sebastopol : Turkish Crimea.

Sinclair, William. Assistant Surgeon.
>Arrived on 13th October, 1854 and left on Medical Certificate on
>21st March, 1855.
>Sebastopol : Turkish Crimea.

McDonald, Alexander. Sergeant.
>Wounded at the Alma.

Ervan, [-]. Private.

McKay, John. Private.
>Wounded at the Alma.

95th Regiment (Derbyshire).

Hume, Henry. Lieutenant Colonel, C.B.
>Commanded 95th at Inkermann. Wounded at the Alma and at
>Inkermann. Returned home on account of wounds on 13th June,
>1855.
>Alma, Inkermann, Sebastopol : C.B. : Knight, Legion of Honour :
>4th Class Medjidie : Turkish Crimea : Brevet Lt. Colonel.

Charlton, Edward Spicer. Captain.
>Alma, Inkermann, Sebastopol : Turkish Crimea.

Garrard, R. Captain.
>Arrived on 14th September, 1854 and returned home on
>21st November, 1854 on Medical Certificate having been wounded
>at the Alma.
>Alma : Turkish Crimea.

Morgan, A. Captain.
>Arrived on 14th September, 1854 and returned home on
>15th December, 1854 on Medical Certificate.

Bazalgette, Evelyn. Lieutenant.
>Arrived on 14th September, 1854 and returned home on
>28th October, 1854 on account of wounds received at the Alma.
>Served again from 4th October, 1855 to 21st January, 1856.
>Alma : Turkish Crimea.

Boothby, Basil Charles. Lieutenant.
>Wounded at the Alma : foot amputated. Returned home
>28th October, 1854.
>Alma : Sardinian War Medal : Turkish Crimea.

Smith, Edmund Davidson. Lieutenant.
>Wound to the head before Sebastopol, 17th October, 1854. Returned
>home on 21st November, 1854 on Medical Certificate.
>Alma, Inkermann, Sebastopol : Turkish Crimea.

Chun, Joseph. Private.
>Wounded at Inkermann.

Haslem, Henry. Private.
>Wounded.

Mullaney, Patrick. Private. Also occurs as Mulloney.
>Wounded.

Murphy, Joseph. Sergeant.
>Wounded at the Alma.

97th Regiment (Earl of Ulster's).

Annesley, William Richard. Captain.
>Arrived 20th November, 1854 and returned home to depot on
>Medical Certificate on 14th December, 1854.
>Sebastopol : Turkish Crimea.

Madden, Daniel. Corporal.
Holbrook, John. Private.
Sergent, Henry. Private.
Taylor, Charles. Private.

The Rifle Brigade.

Bradford, Wilmot Henry. Lieutenant Colonel.
>Arrived on the 14th September, 1854 and left for home (to 3rd
>Battalion) on 9th February, 1855.
>Alma : 5th Class Medjidie : Turkish Crimea.

Horsford, Alfred H. Lieutenant Colonel, C.B.
>Commanded 1st Battalion, 1854. Returned home on Medical
>Certificate on 24th December, 1854.
>Alma, Balaklava, Inkermann, Sebastopol : C.B. : Sardinian War
>Medal : 5th Class Medjidie : Turkish Crimea.

Elliot, Gilbert, the Hon. Brevet Major.
>A.D.C. to Major General Sir George Cathcart; D.A.Q.M.G., 4th
>Division.
>Alma, Sebastopol : Sardinian War Medal : 5th Class Medjidie :
>Turkish Crimea : Brevet Major.

Elrington, Frederick Robert. Major.
>Arrived 14th September, 1854 and returned to England 9th February,
>1855 to join 3rd Battalion.
>Alma, Inkermann, Sebastopol : Knight, Legion of Honour : 5th Class
>Medjidie : Turkish Crimea.

Erroll, William Harry, the Earl of. Brevet Major.
>Severely wounded at the Alma; returned to England in October, 1854
>on account of wounds.
>Alma : 5th Class Medjidie : Turkish Crimea : Brevet Major.

Hardinge, Henry. Major.
>Arrived 14th September, 1854 and returned to England 4th February,
>1855 to Depot.
>Alma, Inkermann, Sebastopol : 5th Class Medjidie : Turkish Crimea.

66

Bourchier, Claud T. Captain.

> A.D.C. to General Torrens. Arrived 14th September, 1854 and returned to England 15th February, 1855 to join Depot.
> Alma, Inkermann, Balaklava, Sebastopol : Victoria Cross : Knight, Legion of Honour : 5th Class Medjidie : Turkish Crimea : Dispatches.

Buller, Coote. Captain.

> Arrived 14th September, 1854 and returned to England 10th November 1854 on account of severe wounds received at Inkermann.
> Alma, Inkermann, Sebastopol : Turkish Crimea

Deedes, William. Captain. 2nd Battn.

> Alma, Inkermann, Sebastopol : Turkish Crimea.

Drummond, A. Captain. 2nd Battn.

> Arrived 3rd December, 1854; returned to England 9th February, 1855 to 3rd Battalion.

Inglis, T. Captain.

> Arrived 14th September, 1854 and returned to England 15th March, 1855 - retired.

Newdigate, Edward. Captain. 2nd Battn.

> Wounded at Inkermann. Arrived 14th September, 1854 and returned to England October, 1854 on account of wounds. Served again between January, and 25th March, 1855.
> Alma, Inkermann, Sebastopol : Knight, Legion of Honour : 5th Class Medjidie : Turkish Crimea.

Nixon, Arthur James. Captain.

> Arrived 14th September, 1854 and returned to England on 9th February, 1855 to join 3rd Battalion.
> Alma, Inkermann, Sebastopol : 5th Class Medjidie : Turkish Crimea.

Ross, John. Captain.

> A.D.C. to Brigadier General Lawrence. Arrived 14th September, 1854 and returned to England on 9th February, 1855; served again from 24th April, to 10th June, 1856.
> Alma, Inkermann, Sebastopol : 5th Class Medjidie : Turkish Crimea.

Rowles, James. Captain.

> Arrived 14th September, 1854 and returned to England on 9th February, 1855 to join 3rd Battalion.
> Alma, Inkermann, Sebastopol : Turkish Crimea.

Warren, Arthur Frederick. Captain.

> Absent with 3rd Battalion, October – December, 1854 and 9th February, – 26th December, 1855.
> Alma, Sebastopol : 5th Class Medjidie : Turkish Crimea.

Lindsay, Henry Gore. Captain. 1st Battn.

> Arrived 14th September, 1854 and returned to England on 1st November, 1854 on Medical Certificate.
> Alma, Sebastopol : Turkish Crimea.

Careless, William. Private 2557.
> Wounded at Inkermann.

Dulahan, T. Private. Also occurs as Dullahan.
> Wounded.

Holdaway, Andrew. Colour Sergeant.

Johnson, James. Sergeant.

Muggridge, William. Sergeant 3499.
> Wounded at Inkermann.

Palmer, Thomas. Private.
> Wounded.

Titcombe, John. Private.

Royal Marine Forces.

Unless otherwise indicated, recipients should be taken to belong to the Royal Marine Light Infantry.

Cox, Edmund Henry. Lieutenant.
> Portsmouth Division, Royal Marine Artillery.
> Sebastopol : 5th Class Medjidie : Turkish Crimea.

McArthur, Edward. Lieutenant.
> Plymouth Division.
> Sebastopol : 5th Class Medjidie : Turkish Crimea.

March, William Henry. Captain.
> Chatham Division.
> Served with the R.M. Brigade before Sebastopol and attached to Light Division of the army at Balaklava and Inkermann. Severely wounded at Inkermann.
> Balaklava, Inkermann, Sebastopol : Sardinian War Medal : Knight, Legion of Honour : 5th Class Medjidie : Turkish Crimea.

Pym, Frederick George. Lieutenant.
> Woolwich Division.
> Served with R.M. Brigade, Sebastopol; attached to Light Division of the Army at Balaklava and Inkermann.
> Balaklava, Inkermann, Sebastopol : Knight, Legion of Honour : 5th Class Medjidie : Turkish Crimea : Dispatches.

Usher, Edward Price. Captain.
> Woolwich Division.
> Sebastopol : Turkish Crimea.

Walton, Francis. Lieutenant.
> Portsmouth Division.
> Sebastopol : 5th Class Medjidie : Turkish Crimea.

Angel, John. Private.
>Plymouth Division. Wounded.

Barnes, Samuel. Private.
>Plymouth Division.

Batchelor, Henry. Colour Sergeant.
>Plymouth Division.

Bates, William. Private.
>Plymouth Division.

Board, George. Private.
>Plymouth Division.

Bunton, John. Private.
>Woolwich Division. He was one from only eight N.C.O.s and men to receive the Naval Long Service & Good Conduct Medal for gallantry, with gratuity, for distinguished service at Inkermann, where he was severely wounded. The list includes Corporal John Prettyjohn, who also received the Victoria Cross, and it is thought that Bunton was awarded his silver medal and Legion of Honour for the same action. He was discharged on medical grounds eights days before the presentation by Queen Victoria.
>Balaklava, Inkermann, Sebastopol : Naval LS & GC : French Legion of Honour, 5th Class : Turkish Crimea (Sardinian type).

Bush, Benjamin. Private.
>Portsmouth Division.

Chase, William. Corporal.
>Portsmouth Division.

Climpston, William. Private.
>Chatham Division.

Edsell, Henry. Sergeant.
>Portsmouth Division.

Elgney, William. Sergeant.
>Royal Marine Artillery.

Farrell, Patrick. Corporal.
>Woolwich Division.

Fletcher, Charles. Private.
>Portsmouth Division.

Flynn, Michael. Bombardier.
>Royal Marine Artillery.

France, Robert. Private.
>Woolwich Division. Wounded.

Goff, Charles. Private.
>Chatham Division. Wounded at the bombardment of Sebastopol harbour forts, 17th October, 1854, serving on HMS *Trafalgar*.

Gooden, Thomas. Private.
Plymouth Division.
Hapgood, George. Private.
Portsmouth Division.
Henson, Frederick. Private.
Chatham Division.
Hewlett, William J. Gunner.
Royal Marine Artillery.
Holyer, William. Lance Corporal.
Chatham Division.
Hutchinson, John E. Private.
Woolwich Division.
Jackson, James. Private.
Chatham Division.
Kennedy, Robert. Gunner.
Royal Marine Artillery.
Lyons, Timothy. Private.
Portsmouth Division.
McClaming, John. Private.
Woolwich Division.
McElroy, John. Private.
Woolwich Division. Wounded.
Melhuish, John. Gunner.
Royal Marine Artillery.
Midgeley, William. Private.
Woolwich Division.
Osborn, George. Private.
Chatham Division.
Quinn, Robert. Private.
Woolwich Division. Wounded.
Richards, Edward. Colour Sergeant.
Plymouth Division. Wounded.
Robinson, Charles. Private.
Woolwich Division. Wounded.
Robinson, William. Private.
Woolwich Division.
Schooling, James. Private.
Chatham Division.
Smith, Edward. Colour Sergeant.
Chatham Division.
Smith, Samuel. Gunner.
Royal Marine Artillery.

Stantiford, John. Private.
> Plymouth Division.

Sutters, Joseph (?Joshua). Private.
> Woolwich Division. Wounded at bombardment of Sebastopol harbour forts, 17th October, 1854.

Tibbs, Edward. Gunner.
> Royal Marine Artillery.

Warenby, William. Private.
> Woolwich Division.

Watts, George. Private.
> Plymouth Division.

Wilson, Robert. Private.
> Woolwich Division. Wounded.

Woods, Robert. Private.
> Woolwich Division.

Woolley, Bernard. Private.
> Portsmouth Division.

The Royal Navy.

Dundas, James Whitley Deans, Sir. Vice Admiral.
> Sebastopol : Grand Cross, Legion of Honour : 1st Class Medjidie : Turkish Crimea.

Dacres, Sydney Colpoys. Captain.
> Served on *Sans Pareil*.
> Sebastopol : C.B. : 3rd Class Medjidie : Turkish Crimea.

Eden, Charles. Captain.
> Served on *London*.
> Sebastopol : C.B. : Turkish Crimea.

Ewart, Charles Joseph Frederick. Captain.
> Served on *Trafalgar*.
> Sebastopol : Knight, Legion of Honour : 5th Class Medjidie : Turkish Crimea.

Graham, C. Captain.
> Served on *Rodney*

Greville, H.F. Captain.
> Served on *Trafalgar*.

Kynaston, A.F. Captain.
> Served on *Spiteful*.

Paulet, G. Lord. Captain.
> Served on *Bellerophon*.

Rogers, H.D. Captain.
> Served on *Albion*.

Russell, E. Lord. Captain.
>Served on *Vengeance*.
>Baltic : Sebastopol : Knight, Legion of Honour : 4th Class Medjidie :
>Turkish Crimea.

Bridge, William Henry. Commander.
>Served on *Vengeance*.
>Sebastopol : Turkish Crimea.

Jones, William Gore. Commander.
>Served on *Firebrand*.
>Sebastopol : Knight, Legion of Honour : 5th Class Medjidie :
>Turkish Crimea.

McDonald, John Wallace Douglas. Commander.
>Sebastopol : 5th Class Medjidie : Turkish Crimea.

Norman, J.N. Commander.
>Served on *Trafalgar*; severely wounded.

Rolland, William Rae. Commander.
>Served on *Agammemnon*.
>Sebastopol : Knight, Legion of Honour : 5th Class Medjidie :
>Turkish Crimea.

Anderson, Warren Hastings. Lieutenant.
>Served on *Sans Pareil*; wounded.
>Sebastopol : Turkish Crimea.

Berkeley, Joshua. Lieutenant.
>Served on *Vengeance*.
>Sebastopol : Turkish Crimea.

Borrett, Thomas. Lieutenant.
>Served on *Britannia*.
>Sebastopol : Turkish Crimea.

Boulton, William Raymond. Lieutenant.
>Served on *Bellerophon*.
>Baltic : Sebastopol : Turkish Crimea.

Bull, James. Lieutenant.
>Served on *Sans Pareil*; severely wounded 17th October, 1854.
>Sebastopol : Knight, Legion of Honour : 5th Class Medjidie :
>Turkish Crimea.

Capel, Randolph Alfred, the Hon. Lieutenant.
>Served on *Britannia*.
>Sebastopol : Turkish Crimea.

Cecil, Edward, Lord. Lieutenant.
>Served on *Leander*
>Baltic : Sebastopol : Turkish Crimea.

Chetwynd, Henry Weyland, the Hon. Lieutenant.
>Served on *Sphynx*.
>Baltic : Sebastopol : Turkish Crimea.

Drake, George Arthur Tyrwhitt. Lieutenant.
>Served on *Arethusa*.
>Baltic : Sebastopol : Turkish Crimea.

Griffiths, J.F. Lieutenant.
>Served on *Britannia*.

Henderson, A. Lieutenant.
>Served on *Sampson*.

Holder, Henry Lowe. Lieutenant.
>Served on *Vengeance*.
>Sebastopol : 5th Class Medjidie : Turkish Crimea

Lambert, L. Lieutenant.
>Served on *Spiteful*.

Nelson, Maurice Horatio, the Hon. Lieutenant.
>Served on *Sampson*.
>Crimea medal, no clasp : 5th Class Medjidie : Turkish Crimea.

Rogers, Henry. Lieutenant.
>Served on *Arethusa*.
>Baltic : Crimea medal with two clasps : Turkish Crimea.

Rolinson, J. Lieutenant.
>Served on *Trafalgar*.

Sullivan, F. Lieutenant.
>Served on *London*.
>Sebastopol : Turkish Crimea.

Taylor, G. Lieutenant.
>Served on *Arethusa*.

Waymouth, W. Lieutenant
>Served on *Sans Pareil*.

Wilberforce, H.W. Lieutenant.
>Served on *Trafalgar*.

Wilson, W.L. Lieutenant.
>Served on *Vengeance* : wounded.

Adams, Allen Crosby. Midshipman.
>Served on *Sans Pareil*.
>Sebastopol : Turkish Crimea.

Digby, Noel Stephen Fox. Midshipman.
>Served on *Britannia*.
>Baltic : No Crimea medal entitlement traced.

Durrant, Francis. Midshipman.
>Served on *Trafalgar*.
>Blatic : Sebastopol : Turkish Crimea.

Flood, Ferdinand Henry Solly. Midshipman.
>Served on *Bellerophon*.
>Sebastopol : 5th Class Medjidie : Turkish Crimea.

Hamilton, Blair Skeffington. Midshipman.
>Served on *Retribution*.

Medlycott, Mervyn Bradford. Midshipman.
>Served on *Bellerophon*
>Baltic : No Crimean medal entitlement traced.

Molyneux, Robert Henry Moore. Midshipman.
>Served on *Sans Pareil*.
>Baltic : Sebastopol : Turkish Crimea.

Stirling, Walter. Midshipman.
>Served on *Britannia*
>Sebastopol : Turkish Crimea.
>Transferred to the Coldstream Guards.

Wingfield, Maurice, the Hon. Midshipman.
>Served on *Vengeance*.

Bremner, John Traill Urquhart. Medical Officer.
>Served on *Sans Pareil*.
>Sebastopol : 5th Class Medjidie : Turkish Crimea.

Graham, W. Doctor. Surgeon.
>Served on *Vengeance*.

Beveridge, Hugh Tod Spalding. Doctor. Surgeon.
>Served on *Sampson*.
>Baltic : Sebastopol : Turkish Crimea.

Creighton, Robert. Assistant Surgeon.
>Served on *Trafalgar*.
>Baltic : Sebastopol : Turkish Crimea.

Hamilton, W. Paymaster.
>Served on *Britannia*.

Bird, Edward Timothy Brown. Engineer.
>Served on *Terrible*.
>Baltic : Sebastopol : Turkish Crimea.

Reynolds, R.C. Engineer.
>Served on *Agammemnon*.

Beard, John. Able Seaman.
>Served on *Retribution*.

Beer, J. Armourer.
>Served on *Sampson*.

Bridget, H. Chief Quartermaster.
>Served on *Bellerophon*.

Brooks, Charles. Admiral's Coxswain.
>Served on *Britannia*.

Brown, Thomas. Chief Quartermaster.
>Served on *Sans Pareil*.
>Sebastopol : Turkish Crimea.

Coakley, Daniel. Gunner's Mate.
>Served on *Britannia*.

Dawe, W. Armourer.
> Served on *Bellerophon*.

Day, Joseph. Able Seaman.
> Served on *Trafalgar*.

Elme, John. Able Seaman.
> Served on *Britannia*.

Fawckner, William Henry. Second Master.
> Served on *Vengeance*.
> Baltic : Sebastopol : Turkish Crimea.

Fost, W.   Leading Seaman.
> Served on *Sans Pareil*.

Foulkes, Charles Kenrick. Clerk.
> Served on *Bellerophon*.

Garland, James. Admiral's Coxswain.
> Served on *Retribution*.

Goulding, John. Able Seaman.
> Served on *Retribution*.

Gribble, James. Able Seaman.
> Served on *Retribution*.

James, J. Captain of Forecastle.
> Served on *Trafalgar*.

Jillard, Jacob. Leading Seaman.
> Served on *Vengeance*.

Joste, J.S. Carpenter's Crew.
> Served on *Sampson*.

Lambe, J.W. Mate.
> Served on *Trafalgar*.

Mason, William. Leading Seaman.
> Served on Arethusa.

Melson, Frederick. Captain of Aftguard.
> Served on *Vengeance*.

Mooney, J. Leading Seaman.
> Served on *Sans Pareil*.

Nicolas, George T. Mate.
> Served on *Retribution*.

Pain, S. Sailmaker's Crew.
> Served on *Bellerophon*.

Parkinson, Charles. Second Master.
> Served on *Sans Pareil*; wounded.
> Sebastopol : 5th Class Medjidie : Turkish Crimea.

Payne, Robert. Leading Seaman.
> Served on *Vengeance*.

Pearce, George. Leading Seaman.
>Served on *Arethusa* and *Rodney*: wounded 18th June, 1855.

Pengelley, E. Leading Seaman.
>Served on *Sans Pareil*.

Ridley, Joseph. Leading Seaman.
>Served on *Trafalga*r.

Rowe, J. Second Captain Foretop.
>Served on *Bellerophon*.

Smith, Charles. Leading Seaman.
>Served on *Trafalgar*.

Starling, J. Boatswain.
>Served on *Sampson*.

Thorne, Thomas. Gunner's Mate.
>Served on *Arethusa*. Wounded 17th October, 1854 at bombardment of Sebastopol harbour forts. Promoted to Bosun's Mate.

Toomey, Michael. Able Seaman.
>Served on *Britannia*.

West, Charles. Leading Seaman.
>Served on *Arethusa*.

Willis, James. Leading Seaman.
>Served on *Vengeance*.